PRO  Y
for
WRITERS

A Writer's Guide to Creating Abundance

HONORÉE CORDER
AUTHOR OF VISION TO REALITY

ALSO BY HONORÉE CORDER

You Must Write a Book: Boost Your Brand, Get More Business
& Become the Go-To Expert

I Must Write My Book: The Companion Workbook to
You Must Write a Book

The Prosperous Writer book series

Prosperity for Writers:
A Writer's Guide to Creating Abundance

Prosperity for Writer's Productivity Journal

The Nifty 15: Write Your Book in Just 15 Minutes a Day!

The Prosperous Writer's Guide to Making More Money:
Habits, Tactics, and Strategies for Making a Living as a Writer

The Prosperous Writer's Guide to Finding Readers:
Build Your Author Brand, Raise Your Profile,
and Find Readers to Delight!

———

Business Dating: Applying Relationship Rules in Business
for Ultimate Success

Tall Order: Organize Your Life and Double Your Success
in Half the Time

Vision to Reality: How Short Term Massive Action Equals
Long Term Maximum Results

The Divorced Phoenix: Rising from the Ashes of a Broken
Marriage

If Divorce is a Game, These are the Rules: 8 Rules for Thriving
Before, During and After Divorce

The Successful Single Mom book series

The Miracle Morning book series

PROSPERITY
FOR
WRITERS

A Writer's Guide
to Creating Abundance

HONORÉE CORDER

Published by Honorée Enterprises Publishing, LLC.

ISBN: 978-0996186117

Discover other titles by Honorée Corder at http://www. honoreecorder.com.

SPECIAL INVITATION

Many like-minded individuals have gathered in an online community to share ideas, render support, and promote accountability. When I first wrote *Prosperity for Writers*, I envisioned helping numerous writers shatter the belief that they must starve to survive. I had no idea what was in store, and the result is an amazing community of 700+ writers, authors, editors, and more!

I'd like to personally invite you to join the The Prosperous Writer Mastermind at HonoreeCorder.com/Writers and Facebook.com/groups/ProsperityforWriters where you will find motivation, daily support, and help with any writing or self-publishing questions.

You can connect with me personally on Twitter @ Honoree, or on Facebook.com/Honoree. Thank you so much for your most precious resource, your time. I look forward to connecting and hearing about your book soon!

GET EVEN MORE

AS A THANK YOU FOR
reading this book, I want to give you a free copy of:

Tall Order! 7 Master Strategies to Organize Your Life and Double Your Success in Half the Time!

This book is packed with advice for business professionals who want to *double* their income and *triple* their time off! Go here and tell me where to send your free book:

http://honoreecorder.com/freetallorder

TABLE OF CONTENTS

INTRODUCTION

In early 2015, I attended the Colonists Summit in Austin, Texas hosted by Sean Platt and Johnny B. Truant. You might know them as the co-hosts, with David Wright, of *The Self-Publishing Podcast*. I spent the weekend with two-dozen writers: established writers, aspiring writers, full-time writers, and part-time writers. What all of us had in common was our love of writing. But the Summit was not about writing. We weren't there to learn how to write, write faster, or even write better. The Colonists Summit was all about marketing. We had come to learn from some of the best in the business about how to market our books better, faster, and smarter. We all wanted more readers, and ultimately, to make more money from our writing as authors.

Even the most accomplished full-time writers of the group wanted to know how to increase their mailing lists, number of readers, and ultimately make more money. Including me.

But before I can even talk about what led me to write this book (from my initial starting point, the conversation that sparked the idea, to here), I'm going to talk for just a minute about me. So, if you have never, ever heard or read anything about me and you're wondering who I am, here goes.

WHO AM I?

My name is Honorée Corder. I've been a self-published, nonfiction writer since 2005, with the release of my first book, *Tall Order!* As of this writing, I have 16 published titles. I sell e-books, audiobooks, paperback books, and even custom printed books. As a business and executive coach, I provide strategic planning and accountability to professionals and senior-level executives. I also do motivational speaking and corporate training. I certify coaches in my business and divorce coaching methods, and I certify facilitators in the Single Mom Transformation Program. After many years, I have created multiple streams of income—several of them stemming from my writing.

But Rome was not built in a day! It has taken me two and a half decades to define, refine, and build my businesses. Some would even say they were built against great odds. It might be important for you to know that I wasn't born with a silver spoon in my mouth—let me be clear, I wasn't. Although I did start with things people might call an advantage, including the fact that I'm tall, and other things people would confirm are definitely disadvantages: I was a foster kid who lived in a children's home, and never made it to college. I was also "given" beliefs about money —some of them helped me to move forward, and some of them held me back.

Because of my own limiting beliefs around writing and making money as a writer, it took me until my seventh book to call myself an author. Even then, I would very quickly disqualify my writing by letting people know I wasn't a *real* writer. I hadn't gone to college and received a degree in English, journalism, or frankly any degree at all … because I never actually went to college. I only wrote my first book because Mark Victor Hansen pointed out to me that the only way for me to establish credibility as a coach and speaker was to author a book. It never even crossed my mind to write a book proposal, find an agent, or approach traditional publishers. I simply didn't think I was good enough to do so. Instead, I self-published. Since it never occurred to me that I was a real writer, I certainly didn't believe I could earn a living from my writing. My own limiting beliefs held me back longer than I would ever have liked, but I digress.

Before I started coaching, speaking, and writing books, I made my first fortune in network marketing in my 20s. The very nature of building a network marketing business requires an individual to focus, in large part, on their personal development. I learned some of the skills I'll be sharing with you in this book over 20 years ago when I was building that business.

When I published *Tall Order!*, I took the advice of my self-appointed mentors Jack Canfield and Mark Victor Hansen and did at least seven things every day to promote and sell my book. By the time I received the first shipment of five thousand books from the printer, I had pre-sold eleven thousand copies. I had no idea at the time that selling that many copies wasn't completely normal. But I had, and held onto, my belief that I wasn't a real author, or even a writer, at all.

Even though I had made relatively substantial money selling a book I had written, I held onto beliefs that did not serve or empower me. It took me several years to work through the stages and steps to become a prosperous writer. I'm going to share with you these same stages and steps and help you navigate them with ease and grace.

My Big Decision & the Five-Year Plan

I celebrated 40 years on this planet in September 2010. At that point, I had published two books. More than 99 percent of my monthly income came from my coaching and speaking business. I was simultaneously tired and inspired. It's not that I didn't want to work; I just didn't want to work as hard as I had been working for the prior two decades. I also noticed that sales from some of my books had steadily increased over time, with little to no effort on my part. With the introduction of digital books, it was easier and faster than ever for readers to discover my work.

Birthdays ending with a zero are sometimes cause for self-reflection, and mine was no different. I could see the writing on the walls, and I even caught glimpses of opportunities that could lie ahead—if I took advantage of them. Enter the five-year plan.

Shortly after my 40th birthday, I decided that by September 2015 I would be making more money from multiple streams of income that did not require my structured, daily attention. My goals included identifying ways to leverage my knowledge and experience. Once I did that and I put out a BOLO (which you will learn about very soon), I started to notice opportunities I had not noticed before. One of those opportunities was to capitalize on the growing success of my book, *The Successful Single Mom*. Once upon a time, I had penciled out several titles to follow that original book. And although I had written, and had at the ready, *The*

Successful Single Mom Cooks! Cookbook, I had failed to publish it in any format (other than to have it available for download as a PDF on my website). Not exactly the best way to market or sell a book, for sure.

The Successful Single Mom book was consistently selling more and more copies every month. In addition, I would receive messages on Facebook, Twitter, and even long, handwritten letters from single moms around the world who had read and loved the book. The first step in executing my five-year plan was to complete the rest of the intended books in the single mom series. So, over the next four years, I did. In addition to that, a family attorney suggested that I begin certifying facilitators so that the class I had originally created for the book (and taught to a handful of single moms) could be available to single moms everywhere. I later wrote *The Successful Single Dad* at the request of yet another divorce attorney, and a few years after that I wrote *If Divorce is a Game, These are the Rules*. I also wrote several business books, including *Vision to Reality, Business Dating*, and a few others.

Every time I took a step in the right direction, another opportunity showed up. And all along the way I had to identify and overcome, the limiting beliefs I had around making money in each of those areas. Through trial and error, bouts of frustration, and a whole lot of commitment to the process, I persevered. And today I am thriving and making more than enough money from my writing. I am a prosperous writer!

WHY WRITE THIS BOOK?

Which brings me back to the Colonists Summit. When I heard some of the other writers, throughout the course of the weekend, express many of the same limiting beliefs I used to have, my first thought was, *No, no, no, that is so not necessary!* Every part of me wanted to jump up and down and yell, "You don't have to struggle! Being miserable isn't necessary! Success, abundance, and prosperity are easier than you think." But I restrained myself, and instead started a dialogue about a book specifically for writers who want to break through their limiting beliefs around making money as writers so that they could finally, *finally*, make a living from their writing.

The idea of a book with this topic was well received by my fellow Summit attendees and other writers I reached out to in the following weeks. I developed the Prosperity for Writers course, which was immensely fun and resulted in some pretty amazing things for the attendees (and me!). Yes, you'll get to read about them in this book. The result of that course is this book (of the same name), and the course is available now as well.

WHY A BOOK ABOUT PROSPERITY AND WRITERS?

In writing this book, I felt that I could help aspiring and published writers alike do three things that would help them massively increase the amount of money they were making (from writing, and other sources as well):

Number one: Give yourself permission to make money as a writer.

For me, this was the first step in increasing my income as a writer. I've provided my own story, as well as the stories of the writers who took the Prosperity for Writers course[1], to help further explain this concept. You'll also get a peek behind the curtain from my interviews with a dozen successful writers about their writing and thought processes to becoming prosperous writers.

I know that what I share with you in this book is all you need to go from a struggling writer to a prosperous writer. I realize what a big promise that is, and I guarantee to deliver on that promise! Within this book is a formula for success that will work, *if* you work it. The action steps are laid out in a way that is simple and easy for you to execute. All you have to do is take action and keep taking action.

It's taken me years to identify and perfect the tools and advice I'm sharing with you in this book—and they are without question the best things I ever did for my businesses, my income, and myself.

---

[1] *For more information about the* Prosperity for Writers course, *visit https://gum.co/P4W2015* and use code "readers" to receive a 50% discount.

Number two: Change the way you feel about money and about making money as a writer.

You might feel confused about money. You may have conflicting beliefs about money, some of which you have yet to identify. You may love and hate money (and people who have it) at the same time or at least in the same day. Conflicting beliefs and attitudes about money create incompatible results. Everything is energy, and money is no different. Wouldn't it be great if you could get to the point where you knew you would always have more than enough money coming to you? And the icing on top of that very delicious cupcake? Money will come to you from doing something you really love: writing.

The ideas, strategies, and action steps I'm going to share with you in this book have the ability to transform not only how you feel about money, but also how you feel about making money as a writer. It is absolutely possible for someone to make an abundance of money from writing. *And right here, right now, that someone is you.*

Number three: Enable you to shift, expand, reverse, or change your beliefs.

Speaking of beliefs, I know it is imperative that you get a handle on yours. This book focuses primarily on how to become a prosperous writer, i.e., making more than enough money from writing. In order to do this *making more money thing* you're going to have to not only identify limiting beliefs you have and eliminate them, but you're also going to have to identify and adopt amazing beliefs that serve you.

Much of this book is dedicated to providing you with tangible, practical, and yes, spiritual concepts, strategies, and ideas that will (if you let them) transform your inner world as much as it transforms your outer bank balance.

This book is *not* a how-to guide to being a better writer. For that, there are many, many books on the subject. A great place to start is with Stephen King's *On Writing*. This book is not going to discuss marketing. You would be well served to read *Write. Publish. Repeat.* by Sean Platt and Johnny B. Truant and *How to Make a Living with Your Writing* and *Business for Authors: How to be an Author Entrepreneur* by Joanna Penn. I won't discuss your professional book cover design, the importance of having multiple editors, proofreaders, or even advanced readers. There's no time to chat about designing your website, or getting the word out about your writing on social media. All of that has been done, and done well, by many of my colleagues. For just the right book on any self-publishing topic, you'll want to visit HonoreeCorder.com/myfavoritebooks and look under self-publishing.

This book *is* a prosperity manual for writers who are struggling or have struggled in any way around making money. It's a reference guide for the writer who has dreams and aspirations of writing stories, articles, nonfiction books, or tomes of any kind in the hopes of reaping a satisfying financial reward and living abundantly. It is a heart project from an author who desires to see everyone who wants to make a living from doing what they love be able to do just that.

If you are an aspiring writer, or even someone who makes an abundance of money from writing—just not writing what you truly want to write—this book can help you too, and that's why I wrote it. I know it can help you break through your blocks and beliefs around money and help you make the leap to full-time, prosperous writer.

I hope you enjoy the book, the stories of your fellow writers, and everything I'm sharing with you. My hope is that it inspires you to become the prosperous writer you've always wanted to be.

Are you ready?

YOU CAN BE A PROSPEROUS WRITER!

Yes, you! The process of transitioning from a struggling to a prosperous writer is simpler and easier than you most likely *think* or *believe* currently. I'm excited you picked up this book, because we are going to go on a journey together, and on this journey you have the opportunity to go from where you are now to where you want to be in a *very* short period of time. You'll have more fun than you might think, with less effort than you can possibly imagine, *all while making more money.*

I know that sounds like an incredibly big promise. It is. And I'm excited to make that promise because I've made it and kept it many times before. I've been living it. By living it, I mean I have consistently worked on and through all of the practices, ideas, and suggestions I'm sharing with you in this book. I have kept my promise by sharing the time-tested strategies I discovered and developed with my friends, clients, and students of various classes. I've helped them become more prosperous than they ever dared to hope. I know these strategies work because I've done this on multiple occasions and in numerous ways. I understand completely if you have doubts and hesitations; I would too if I were you. Let me help assuage your doubts by sharing a testimonial from a skeptical student from the Prosperity for Writers course.

Ephraim was incredibly hesitant to even participate in the class because he had tried other classes and methods and had consulted with multiple teachers and coaches ... all without the results he wanted. I didn't want Ephraim to participate in the class if he wasn't going to fully participate, because I have always had a 100 percent success rate. I reminded Ephraim, "I have a perfect record, and I'm not going to let you screw it up. I need you to commit wholeheartedly to this program." And here's what he had to say after taking my class:

I've been writing! The best part: I've been writing even more than I imagined. I write longhand and at my computer. I'm working on multiple projects. And ideas have been flowing—including solutions for tricky plot puzzles and nonfiction conundrums that need to be explained in exactly the right way. It's the magic that I always expected, but sabotaged with my inconsistency. Now I'm here, at the page, every day, savoring every precious drop of creative ecstasy. At last, my muses know where to find me. Or, more likely, I know where to find them.

I wasn't being cheeky or arrogant about my success rate. I know the tools I share are effective, and I do know they will work for you. Because you picked up this book, I know you hold at least a tiny shred of hope that there is a possibility you can earn a living from your writing, and that you can become, as many others have before you, a prosperous writer. But hope is not a strategy, and hope won't pay the rent while you write. You need tangible action steps, and I'm going to share the best I've got with you.

While a prosperous writer is someone who either can, or does, support themselves with their writing, they sometimes choose to continue to work in another vocation or job that pays the bills while developing a writing career. At some point they realize they could quit their day job, but they don't, either because they enjoy their job, or they aren't quite comfortable enough with their financial situation to make the leap. Other times, writers earn money from multiple sources—not just from their writing. Finally, there are writers who support themselves and sometimes even their families solely from the proceeds of their writing.

Joanna Penn recently released a brilliant book, *How to Make a Living with Your Writing*. In it she shares,

> *There have been a number of surveys in recent years that report the average income for authors. Most range between $5,000 and $30,000 per year. That's not what I call a living. In my experience, if you want to make a decent living, you have to develop multiple streams of income.*

I completely agree! In my case, I am a serial entrepreneur. I do business coaching and certify coaches in my coaching method. I am a speaker and do more than a dozen trainings and keynotes each year. I also write books and project manage a series of books that I do not write. It has taken some time, and quite a bit of effort for sure, to develop multiple streams of income. While at this point I could live off of any one of them, I thoroughly enjoy being involved in multiple endeavors. It's been an interesting journey from defining what I wanted from writing (be a published author) to making an abundant living as a writer. And I'll share the pieces with you.

My guess is that you picked up this book because you are ready to earn enough money as a writer to fully support yourself and your family. Whether or not you choose to do this is up to you. In my mind, that would make you ready to become a prosperous writer. A full-time, multiple-streams-of-income, royalty-earning, published author. And, if that's what you have in mind, let's keep going!

Permission to Make Money as a Writer

In 2014, I wrote a book for businesspeople called *Vision to Reality*. In it, I talk about four things that precede a fully realized vision. I know that in order to go from *If I am a writer, I will be poor* to *I am a successful, prosperous author"* is a bit of a trek. On that trek, there are four mental hurdles that you must leap over before you will be able to live the vision of becoming the prosperous author you hold in your mind. They are: *think, believe, deserve*, and *commit*.

I will be exploring all four of them with you in this book because I want you to get to your end result: making more and more money as a writer, as quickly as possible.

The first of these benchmarks, *think*, is also the first step on your journey to being a prosperous author. Indeed, you must *think* you can be a prosperous author in order to be one. Sounds simple, doesn't it? But right now, could you see yourself among the group of people (of which there are many) who make a substantial living as writer? If so, congratulations! You've checked the first box on the road to becoming a rich writer.

But *think* is where many people actually start *and* stop. So I'm going to spend a few moments right here for the person who is stuck at *think*. You might be a person who can't even conceive, for even a moment, that it's possible for you to truly make a living from writing. You might be thinking, *Who am I to think that I can make a living from my writing?* Let me address that by asking,

"Why not?" There's a reason you love to write. Almost every time I speak to a writer, hear an interview, or read a book written by a writer (obviously), I hear that they are literally compelled to write. *They must write*, and they love it! I believe if you feel compelled to write, you should write. And if you love to write, you should write. I also believe you deserve to make money from your writing. But I'm getting a little ahead of myself.

I want the world to challenge and change its assumption that writers should struggle by virtue of their choice to write—just as I want you to challenge and change your assumption that you can't be a prosperous writer (and you won't allow yourself to *think* you can) as well.

Perhaps you think that no one would want to read what you have to write. All right, I totally understand. The first thing I feel compelled to point out to you is that there are, give or take, eight billion people living on planet Earth. The chances that even a fraction of them would want to read your writing is *pretty* darn good. And, the chances that they would pay to read your words? Also pretty good. The way I see it, you have an audience of people waiting to hear what you have to say. Don't make them lose out because you're holding yourself back. In my mind that would be tragic! Can you go with me on this? Excellent!

Since you're still with me, I'm going to assume you can now *think* that it is possible for you to earn a living as a writer. True? Can you entertain it as a possibility?

That's all we need right now: to open that door of possibility, just a crack.

Wealthy people have *wealthy people settings*, and what that means, in part, is that they have money and they believe they will always have money. Prosperous authors have *prosperous author settings*, and, you guessed it, what that means is they believe they are able to make money from their writing, and, of course, that their books *will sell*. You may have a belief that says, *I can make money, plenty of money in fact, just not from my writing*. If that is the case, you don't have the right setting yet, but stay with me here! Whatever belief you have right now is okay because you can change your settings (beliefs) at any time. In fact, that is the first thing I want this book to do for you.

You might need a small shift. Even one degree of difference in your thinking and belief systems can radically transform your outcome. In, of course, the best way. If you're thinking to yourself, *Gosh, I've been struggling with this my whole life; I probably need a complete overhaul*, that's okay too. We are going to get all of that handled. Before you know it, maybe even within the next 24 hours, you will see the benefits of a shift in your thinking.

Here is an important thing to notice: you are here, you have the time to read, and you have the money to buy this book. That tells me a few things about you: you're already making money from other sources—maybe even from writing—which means you're taken care of. Whether you're barely paying the bills or making copious amounts of money from doing what you don't love, either situation tells me that your basic setting (as of right now) is that your basic needs are met. And that, my friend, is a terrific place to start.

Without even realizing it, you've already taken the first important step to shifting your beliefs and making more money as a writer: you bought this book. You may feel like you are in a dark place when it comes to making money from your writing. But here's some great news for you; dark places don't stay dark when you shine a light on them. Acknowledging that where you are is different from where you want to be takes tremendous courage! This initial effort should not go unacknowledged or unnoticed. Give yourself a high five or smack on the ass, whatever you need, and let's keep going.

INTERESTED OR COMMITTED?

I want to set an important expectation for you right away. The expectation is that you are going to get exactly what you put into this process, and nothing more. And make no mistake; there is a *huge* difference between being interested in something and being committed to it. If you are merely interested in considering that *maybe,* you could make some more money from your writing, I can tell you right now what will most likely happen next: your lizard brain, the part of the brain that rules from a place of scarcity and fear (the one that shouts: "Your very survival depends upon what you do next!"), will come up with all kinds of reasons why the things I am suggesting are crazy. It will tell you that the practices I've suggested are just *not* for you, or that they'll take up too much time. Your lizard brain will tell you that you should really be doing something else, anything else, besides pursuing a career as an author.

Trust me; you can come up with all sorts of stories and excuses about why what I'm sharing with you isn't going to work for you. You could be saying, "I'm special," "I'm too busy," or "This just won't work for me," or whatever. I've seen before what happens when someone is merely interested in getting an end result, and the difference in the results that occur when they are truly committed. Like I said, I have a 100 percent success record, and I need you to fully commit to this process so a major win-win can occur: I can keep my streak going, and you can become a prosperous writer. Are you up for that?

LET'S TALK ABOUT COMMITMENT

When you commit to something 100 percent, the results can be remarkable. One decision to commit will transform not only your writer income, but also your life! A 100 percent commitment means there is no other option. There is no other path, and there is no other outcome you are willing to settle for. Please, please, do *not* settle. Do not settle for less than everything you want. Do not settle for the life of a struggling writer; you don't need to or have to. I promise. You deserve everything your heart desires, and I believe it would be a travesty to accept anything less.

What I'm going to share with you are practices that are interesting, effective, and fun. They have the potential to completely rock your world in an awesome way. This is where your commitment comes in: you have to be willing to actually *do* them. You have to be willing to do whatever is necessary (within reason, while maintaining your integrity) to make the change or changes you need to make. These changes must occur, both practically and mentally, in order to get the results you want.

I promise that when you integrate the practices I share with you in this book, your ability to earn a significant income from your writing as a published author will be markedly increased. So my question to you is: are you interested, or are you committed?

Know this—the instant you decide something, you step over the line. As a matter of fact, the instant you *decide* you're going to be a prosperous writer, you set the wheels in motion for the manifesting, magic, and miracles to start happening! You are instantly shifted into making, earning, and manifesting more money, right now. I'll get to the *how* shortly. For the moment, stay with me—we have some important ground to cover first.

KEEP THESE TOP OF MIND

I advise you to keep a few things top of mind as you embark upon your transformation to becoming a prosperous writer.

One: There are naysayers out there. Seventy percent of people hate their job. Some of these people might be your friends, your boss, or even your spouse. They don't hate it enough to do anything about it, and they will strongly discourage *you* from doing anything about it either. A fearless and public declaration of, "I am going to write until I can replace my income and escape this miserable job—and I'm damn excited about it!" will be met with some perhaps well-meaning yet still discouraging words. Which leads me to …

Two: Keep quiet about your transformation, the big goals you've set, and your intended outcomes. We all have a need to express what we're excited about, and there's a time, place, and person perfect for you to do so. Express your intention to the wrong person, and they will discourage you. That can be enough to take the wind out of your sails. Avoid the naysayers—the people who are certain they are telling you the hard truth for your own good and giving you a dose of "reality" to help you avoid getting hurt. They might be well meaning, but they won't be helpful. Which brings us to …

Three: If you are struggling with earning money as a writer, chances are you've been programmed to believe you must work hard in order to make money or that writing is a poor man's endeavor. Believing that you must struggle does not serve you; so let that **shitake** go right now! I challenge you to be a light and to be an example to others around you about what is possible. Remember this: you can light all of the other candles in the world with your one candle. You don't have to—you get to! Isn't that exciting?

THE MYTH OF THE STARVING ARTIST

The belief that artists must starve and sacrifice for their art is a real thing. Unfortunately, it is a *real* belief—a socially accepted construct, not just in the United States where I live, but also in countries around the world. In our minds, we seem to picture writers as homeless-looking, unshaven men toiling away, all the while chain smoking, overeating, drinking booze, and struggling ... usually in a very messy room. On rare occasions, there is a shining star that makes his way to the top and finds fame and fortune in his work ... but that is not what our society, or any other society, seems to picture when it comes to artists. In fact, I conducted interviews with several now-prosperous writers who told me they didn't initially even attempt to make a living as a writer because they didn't think it was possible.

My research for this book, and the Prosperity for Writers course, uncovered this unfortunate, and rather disturbing, portrayal of the starving artist:

A starving artist is an artist who sacrifices well-being in order to focus on their artwork. They typically live on minimum expenses, either for a lack of business or because all of their disposable income goes toward art projects. Some starving artists desire mainstream success, but have difficulty due to the high barriers to entry in the arts. These artists frequently take temporary positions such as "waitering," or other service industry jobs, while they focus their attention on breaking through in their preferred field. Others may find enough satisfaction in living as an artist that they choose voluntary poverty— regardless of prospects of future financial reward or broad recognition. —Wikipedia

In a word, yuck! When I read that I felt a combination of anger, sadness, and shock. I'm angry because anything that is accepted as gospel isn't usually challenged or changed. It saddens me that someone would feel like they have to take a vow of poverty in order to be creative. I also have a ton of shock that *literally* millions upon millions of people would buy into that!

Starving artists, and therefore starving writers, have become a cultural given. But why? *Why* do we believe that artists must be starving? Or even, *why* being a creative person means you must be broke or struggling? I'm not sure who started it really, but one of my major goals for this book is to stop it. I want to challenge the status quo and cause the world, starting with you, to stop and think about the assumptions that have been made. Finally, I want those assumptions to change—

starting as soon as possible. How about right now, with you?

Is the belief, *I must strain, strive, and struggle as a writer,* true? I don't think so. Is it true for you? I hope not! I would never ask you to just take my word for something. I want you to really think about what I'm saying, and determine if it applies to you. While the media casts a bright light on a few shining stars who have found fame and fortune in their writing, such as: Stephen King, E.L. James, J.K. Rowling, and most recently Mark Dawson (who was profiled on Fortune. com for making almost a half million dollars in 2014 on Kindle). What you don't hear about all the time are regular folks who make a very nice living (thank you very much) from their writing. These writers are known as mid-listers, are relatively unknown, and make up the majority of earners in the prosperous writing space.

You can view Hugh Howey's Author Earnings Report (at AuthorEarnings.com) to see what writers are making, and this references self-published authors alone. It doesn't reflect the incomes of copywriters, freelance writers, or traditionally published authors who also make a living.

Based on my research and the conversations I've had with dozens and dozens of prosperous writers, I concluded this long-standing and closely-held belief is entirely false. There are currently too many people making a living from their writing for this belief to be true. When we, for even a moment, truly believe that writers must struggle financially, it affects, informs, and influences what we do and don't do. Would you join me in disputing this belief? For the duration of this book I ask that you consider what you may have accepted as a truism is actually untrue.

Let's face it—if I think, after a mountain of hard work and time invested, that I won't get a return on my efforts, I'm likely to not even begin it all. But if I really want something and I believe if I put in the necessary time, effort, and even money, that I can get the results I want, then I am more likely to give it a shot. What about you?

If you have been living under the assumption that you could never be more than a struggling writer, then this assumption has most likely been your reality—if you have given it a shot. Can I get you to suspend your beliefs for a moment and entertain the thought that you, yes you, could make a living as a writer?

Could you replace old beliefs with new ones? Try something like this from Kari Kilgore, graduate of the Prosperity for Writers course:

I am a writer. I write genre agnostic speculative fiction for enthusiastic readers who want thoughtful entertainment. I make an abundant living writing genre agnostic speculative fiction for enthusiastic readers who want thoughtful entertainment.

You'll learn in an upcoming chapter how to create a new, empowering belief to replace old ones that don't serve you. You will soon know how to identify and insert a new empowering belief for just about anything!

This includes making money (an abundant living if you so desire) as a writer.

I might be getting a little ahead of myself, but frankly, this is a topic I'm completely passionate about: helping my fellow writers create the professional lives and incomes they want. But before we get into all of the life-changing goodness that is included in this book, let's address a question I'm sure you have in your mind.

What Is a Prosperous Writer, Anyway?

I believe a prosperous writer is someone who makes a living, a very nice living, from his or her writing. Now, you don't have to make money only from your writing, but you can if that's what you want. In other words, you don't need to stay in a soul-killing job to pay the bills, while writing in the wee hours of the morning, during your lunch break, or after the kids have gone to bed if that isn't what you want. You may have a different definition, and that's awesome. Being a prosperous writer is subjective—prosperous and abundant are in the eyes of the person holding their wallet. Ask any person what a lot of money is, and every single person will have a different answer. Only you know your answer. The entire purpose of this book is to help you define not only what prosperous is, but also what being a prosperous writer is for you and to help you achieve it. In record time, I might add.

Lest you think this journey is going to be easy-peasy or that there won't be some significant work and thought on your part, let's clear that up right now. Depending upon how far you have to go from struggling to abundant and prosperous, there may be quite a bit of time and effort to be put in on your part. You'll have to dig deep, define what you truly want, and be willing to do the inner and outer work required to make the hop or leap needed. The process and work may not always be pretty, but I can assure you it will be worth it.

THE PROSPEROUS WRITER STAGES

There are three distinct stages on the journey to becoming a prosperous writer:

PHASE I: THE WORK HARD PHASE

This phase is without a doubt the most intense, labor-concentrated, frustrating, and least fun phase of all. Which is why a lot of people never make it to Phase II. The Work Hard Phase is tough with a capital "T." In this phase, you are doing everything you can to get to the place where you can be a full-time writer. This includes working on your skills (and there are *a lot* of skills), expanding your mindset (including your beliefs, attitude, and self-confidence), and getting clear on your personal spiritual beliefs.

You may end up taking a three-year temporary position at Starbucks, like writer Bryan Cohen did.

While he is now a full-time writer, author of multiple books including *Ted Saves the World*, and cohost of *The Sell More Books Show*, in his early days he juggled a full-time job while he developed his process, skills, and beliefs about himself and what was possible.

You may go four years without two days off in a row before you finally take a *real* vacation, like Sean Platt of *The Self-Publishing Podcast*. On the verge of creating a full-scale global empire, Sean worked six- and seven-day weeks, including major holidays like Groundhog Day and Christmas, in order to get through the Work Smart Phase and on to the Full-time Writer Phase. As Sean so elegantly said,

> *There is no shortcut, no impending lightning-strike caused by a 'build it and they will come' legend. Writing is a business and you have to be willing to put in the work.*

PHASE II: THE WORK SMART PHASE

This phase is a little more fun, but make no mistake my friend, it is still incredibly intense and massively labor-intensive. Put another way: the words don't write themselves. Navigating your way through Phase I comes with some of the benefits you get to enjoy in Phase II: you will know the hacks, shortcuts, tools, and other ways to get to your goal of being a prosperous writer. You'll discover when and how you do your best writing. You'll define your avatar or "ideal reader" and you'll figure out ways to get yourself to write when writing is the last thing you want to do. Phase II is where you start to gain traction, and you'll see more money and more results than ever before. The byproduct is an uptick in your confidence as well as your income. In this phase you are seeing results, making progress and some money, and have most likely found your groove.

I have two words for you: *keep going.*

PHASE III: THE FULL-TIME WRITER PHASE

You've made it! Or, at least your bank account is telling you there is more money than last month, all of your needs are met, and there is plenty to spare. (Big exhale.) Plus, you are now free to write as much as you choose, every single day. Oh wait, now you're free to write as much or as little as you choose, every single day!

While you now are in the glorious position to have time and money freedom with which to write your little heart out, make no mistake—it is still *on!* You must continue to schedule writing most (if not every) days of the week. Almost no one writes one book and enjoys mega success with recurring income. Just as you publish one book, you must be working on the next one. Write a book. Publish that book. Rinse. Repeat. This success formula is the only way to get to and stay in the Full-Time Writer Phase!

If you're like I was when I embarked on my five-year journey, I wanted to get into (and stay in) the Full-time Writer Phase as quickly, painlessly, and as easily as possible. It took longer than I wanted it to, required more work than I thought it would, and I got less sleep than was ideal, but I made it. And every single inch of my journey was worth it. My goal with this book is to help you do it, too.

Before we continue, I would be remiss as your prosperity coach if I didn't (a) alert you that something cool is *coming soon*, and (b) give you some homework.

Important note: all of the activities, practices, and homework I give you within these pages is meant to bring *increase* to you, not take anything away from you. In other words, the time you invest in these practices will actually give you more time, not take away time. Keep reading; you'll see what I mean.

Let's start with the cool thing first. Something amazing is going to happen to you, for you, and/or with you within the next 24 hours. For real! In the past 20 years, I have led quite a few prosperity classes in one form or another. Although you are not technically taking a class, you are opening your mind to the possibility of something more for yourself, and that opening is all you need to start the money ball rolling right to your front door. So let's just say you're a student of prosperity— and every single one of my students has manifested something cool, amazing, or downright miraculous within the first 24 hours of being exposed to this type of work. Keep your eyes and ears peeled; it's coming! When it happens, you'll want to be sure to have done your homework ...

Homework:

And, your homework is easy! Get a journal, a special prosperity journal just as a companion for reading this book: your own prosperity project. You'll use it to do all of the exercises contained in this book, capture ideas, make notes, and finally, keep track of money, magic, and miracles. You can even get the companion to this book, the *Prosperity for Writers Productivity Journal* here: http://tinyurl.com/prodjournal

If you're ready, let's proceed!

2

PROSPEROUS WRITERS BELIEVE THEY CAN

Every big name author once had a dream to make a living from their writing. The people who dominate both the traditional and self-published headlines of today weren't household names until they had been writing for quite some time. And by time, I mean *years and years.* In most cases, they had written hundreds of thousands of words and published quite a lot of work before hitting the big time. It is easy to believe someone who is financially successful as a writer is a unicorn; a truly special being or a mythical creature who has a special gift and lives under a shining star. Would you be surprised to learn that they are, in fact, none of these? When I figured that out, I was pretty damn excited! I hope you are, too, because you could be a big name author sometime in the future, as well ...

Newsflash: Every single successful writer is a person—just a person, like you and me. Nothing more or less. What separates the ultra successful from the moderately successful and unsuccessful isn't magic fairy dust. No "abracadabra" or magic potion was involved. I've shared the three phases, and without a doubt, every single successful writer has navigated through them magnificently. Just like the successful writers you know about and admire, you'll have to sharpen your skills, put in your time, and take the journey. There is no shortcut or easy button, so you will need to commit to your success—just like those who have traveled the path to writing success before you.

But if I have my way, you'll have an easier time of it, and your journey won't take as long as it's taken others. While I don't think there are shortcuts and I do believe the words don't write themselves (although that would be pretty cool wouldn't it?), I think, scratch that, I *know* there are ways to make the journey to success faster, less stressful, and more pleasurable. Sound good?

I've addressed why *thinking* you can achieve your desired end result of earning a prosperous living as a writer is key. And, while it's one thing to think you can, it's quite another to believe you can. The second step on the journey from aspiring writer to prosperous writer is *belief*. I've hinted about beliefs, and this is the section you've been waiting for that will show you how to get yours in prosperous order.

You Must Believe

Let's start with what you believe right now about making money as a writer.

Hopefully you have done your homework and gotten a prosperity journal, because you're going to need one! In it, you're going to track your progress, capture distinctions, make notes, and discoveries … starting right now, so grab it (and be sure to keep it with you at all times from now on).

In your prosperity journal, write down what you believe right now about making money. Perhaps you believe that it's okay to make plenty of money, and you might even be making plenty of money from something other than writing. You might, like a lot of the world, believe that making money from writing is not possible, is not achievable for you, or is simply something that someone else gets to do.

Imagine all of your beliefs are tabletops. Beliefs, like tabletops, require support. This support may look like evidence that the belief is true. Let's say that you have a belief that's limiting, such as, *I cannot make enough money to support myself from my writing*, and the evidence you see is: (1) the fact that you are indeed not making

25

money from writing, (2) you have attempted to make money from writing in the past and failed, and (3) you don't know anyone personally who actually supports themselves full-time from writing.

It looks like there is strong evidence supporting your belief, and yet, upon closer inspection, you may discover there is evidence that supports the contradictory belief, *I can make enough money to live on from my writing.* But, you ask, "How do I get from a limiting belief to a belief that is unlimited, one that empowers and inspires me?"

I'm so glad you asked! Here goes:

The process of replacing a limiting belief with a new fantastic belief is simple, yet profound. The goal is to literally replace the limiting belief with an empowering belief, and give this new belief some new legs (evidence) to stand on. To do that, you will work your way through the following exercise. Pull out your prosperity journal. Write your old belief at the top of a page, and right under your old, limiting belief, answer the following four questions in this order:

Number one: Is this belief the truth?

Number two: Why is it false?

Number three: How do you feel when you think that belief is true?

Number four: How do you feel when you think it is false?

Number five: What can your new truth be?

I'll give you a hint: if you hold a limiting belief, *it is not the truth*. By its very definition, it is false. You might have to take my word for it at first, but I believe that since I'm the author that makes me the expert, right? Right! Anyway, your job now is to answer the question, "Why is it false?" Your belief isn't true, and you need to answer why it isn't.

Next, and I'll give you another hint, is to answer the question, "How do you feel when you think that belief is true?" It's probably somewhere between bad and really awful. I mean seriously, how can a limiting belief make you feel good in any way? I know, it can't. Yet you need to answer the question anyway because we have to scramble your brain a little (i.e., cause some pain) to open it up long enough for you to change your belief.

Now that your brain is open, it's time to answer the question, "How do you feel when you think it is false?" This time, the answer will probably be between good and fantastic. When you open the door to the possibility that limiting beliefs aren't true, it is normal to get excited! And while you're in that state of excitement, you are ripe to design, define, and adopt a shiny, brand-new belief that you will feel amazing about.

Your final question is, "What could my new truth be?" Any new belief you want to adopt must be crafted from a state of positive expectancy and anticipation. If you aren't quite in the mood to define or crystalize a new belief, you will want to either wait until you are or get yourself there by any means necessary. My triggers for a good mood, in no particular order, are dark chocolate, handwritten notes that come in the mail, a brand new Apple product, comedy shows, great music, or a conversation with someone I love and trust who just happens to be rocking a fantastic attitude. The best, easiest, and fastest way to put yourself in a great mood is to talk to someone in a great mood!

When you are in the place of hope, joy, and positive energy (and nothing less), sharpen your pencil and write down a new truth. This new truth if it were your real-life reality today, would be the most amazing reality possible. Right?!

Experts will tell you that there are two ways to truly change a belief: undergo a significant emotional event or through continuous repetition of that belief until it takes hold. Since I can't give you a significant emotional event to change your belief in an instant, we're going to have to opt for Plan B: continuous repetition. In order for your new belief to become your reality, it needs to be spoken aloud, memorized, repeated, and internalized until it becomes not just something you say or think, but your real life—a new reality.

Because you've taken the time to carefully craft your new belief, your *new truth*, all you have to do is repeat it to yourself day in and day out until you *believe* it. While it's not really that simple, it is almost that simple. There is one tiny extra action you must do to reinforce and even accelerate turning the belief you've written down into your actual belief, and that is to combine this affirmation with a visualization. This step is very simple—all you have to do is take that new truth and turn it into a quick mental movie that you run simultaneously as you're saying the affirmation.

The fastest and easiest way to turn your new identified belief into a belief you *own* is to spend a few minutes every day saying the affirmation out loud while you simultaneously run your mental movie. You want to be sure that your new truth/affirmation is written as though it is happening right now, in real time.

Let me clarify. If you write down something future focused, like, "I look forward to having an abundance of income from my writing," or "I will have an income in excess of $15,000 per month from my writing," you are reinforcing something's happening in the future. Instead, make your statements reflect a reality that is already in existence. For example, "I am so happy and grateful now that I make an abundance of money from my writing," or "Wow, it's so very cool that every month I make more than $15,000 from my writing." You can say them like you're telling your best friend or your mom (and only if they are truly supportive of and awesome about your aspirations).

Do you see the difference? Some people call this fake it till you make it. I wouldn't suggest you run around telling people you're making $15,000 when you're making $15. There's no faking here. What you are doing, my friend, is programming your subconscious mind and adopting a belief that you are making, for example, $15,000 a month from your writing. The subconscious mind is a powerful beast, and programmed correctly, that beast works on your behalf in a pretty awesome way.

So to recap, if you haven't already, eliminate your old "truth" and craft a new truth. Then, program your subconscious mind by saying and simultaneously visualizing your new truth as your current reality.

During my *Prosperity for Writers* course, I asked participants to write down what their current belief was about making money as a writer, and then share what they changed their belief to.

LESLIE WATTS

An author, blogger, co-captain of Writership, co-host of *The Writership Podcast*, and the founder of Empathy Farming.

OLD BELIEFS:

1. *It (meaning making a prosperous living writing books) works for some, but not necessarily me.*

2. *I have a lot of genuine obstacles.*

3. *I believe that I can't both raise my children the way I want and pursue my writing business the way I want.*

NEW BELIEFS:

1. *Of course I can make a prosperous living writing books because I am committed to doing what it takes every day!*

2. *There may be challenges, but I am committed to overcoming them!*

3. *I can be a stellar parent and author because I bring all of my focus to parenting when I'm with my kids and to my writing business when I write.*

KEVIN TUMLINSON

A Wordslinger—Author, blogger, and host of the *Wordslinger Podcast*. He has more than 20 fabulous fiction books available, and truly dislikes pants.

OLD BELIEFS:

My old belief was that making money as a writer meant I had to do drudgery work that sucked the soul out of me. I believed that if I was enjoying the work, it couldn't be the right thing to do. So I would put aside my passion work in favor of copywriting jobs that paid the bills (barely), but did nothing for my personal energy.

New Beliefs:

Now I'm shifting away from that idea entirely. In fact, since I've changed my thinking on this, I've seen more financial growth for my creative writing than I ever saw before. I mean it—I've literally plotted it on a graph, and I can see my income SPIKE at the time when I changed my perspective on all of this.

I'm now moving into a new phase, as well. I've dreamt of doing certain projects and working in certain areas of the industry. My profile, for example, is geared entirely toward the same copywriting and marketing work I've always done, rather than the creative work I want to do. Basically, I keep telling the Universe, "Here I am ... just a copywriter and marketing expert, and that's all I'll ever be!" The same is true with my personal website.

So I'm pulling out the stops on both—retooling them to reflect the life I want rather than the one I've always had, and blasting forward in a whole new adventure!

My old beliefs worked fantastic for keeping me at exactly the spot where I was. My new beliefs will work even better for propelling me forward into my dream life and career, because they'll actually have my passion and energy behind them!

Christina Culbertson

A fantastic assistant, aspiring author, and current psychology graduate student.

Old beliefs:

1. *People who have money are not good people.*
2. *I must work hard for the money I earn, and it will not be easy.*
3. *I need to work in other areas to earn enough money, i.e. "writing" is not enough.*
4. *Money equals time.*

New beliefs:

1. *Good people do good things, regardless of their wealth. I am worthy of abundance and will do "good" with the money I earn.*
2. *Money comes easily and frequently to me, and I take pride in my work.*
3. *I am worth the money I need. My work is worth it, and people want/need it.*
4. *My time is precious, and it does not delegate how much money I make. I can make money with ideas, gifts, words ... anything I put my mind to!*
5. *Money is just an outward presentation of my beliefs. I choose to believe in abundance, and that is what I now see.*

Since changing these beliefs you can bet I've been challenged! But my whole world is changing at the moment, and for the better!

After the Course I started thinking "what if" about more space for our home life and work. Now we are looking at a house to sign a lease, and it's HUGE! I've also noticed that even though I've been paying off all our bills, there is somehow still money in the bank.

I have been more intentional and generous in my giving, (money and other items) and the Universe has always replaced that with more! On rough days I choose to see abundance everywhere I go ... in the air I breath, leaves on the trees, and things everywhere. Thanks to my awesome-sauce boss, I'm also writing more. Creatively, strategically, journaling, and brainstorming. It feels like my ideas are endless, and all I have to do is choose which ones to work on.

You're right! When you're in the flow, things just work better. Everything. I know now that I am creating the reality I live in, and if I want to change it I just need to have the right attitude and action.

WENDY NOLIN

Honorée Certified Coach and Author of *The Top 10 Best Investments in Yourself.*

OLD BELIEF:

My belief about making money as a writer was that it's totally possible, but not as much as I think, would like, or as fast.

New belief:

My belief now is that I can always get more or make more money as a writer, and there's more where it came from. There is plenty for everyone, including me, and it is coming now, in large amounts. As I spend, I earn double.

Since adopting this new belief, my current writing project has expanded and the manuscript is approaching 25 to 30K words with a level of depth, meaning, and purpose that I've never felt. I am attracting more coaching clients and am approaching a record season (summer is typically the slowest time of the year) with regard to revenue. As a result, I have also closely examined my brand to attract my ideal clients through podcast interviews, article contributions, and a book launch campaign.

Any questions? I'm guessing you want to do a little belief changing of your own. I'll wait, take your time—this is important work you're doing! When you're ready, let's keep going.

You Must Believe ... You Deserve What You Want

Next, (and this is a big one) you have to believe you deserve to make a living, a really, really, *really* good living, as a writer. I spend a lot of time working with my coaching clients on the concept of *deserving*. I call it "deserve-ability," and what that means to me is the ability to believe you deserve what you say you want. How much do you desire to make a prosperous living as a writer? Do you believe you deserve to make $50,000 a year as a writer? And is that enough to support you? How about $100,000 a year? How about $500,000 a year? Or even $1 million?

Many people get stuck between believe and deserve. It is more common than you think. But this is about you, and only you, and if you don't close the gap between belief and deserve, you'll continue to stay right where you are: wanting more, but not getting it. Like a thermostat set at 72 degrees when you start to make money, something will happen to take you back to where you believe you deserve to be. Conversely, if you're not making enough, something will happen that will bring you back up to your 72 degree setting, also known as your current status quo.

Similar to adopting any belief you want to, you can believe you deserve whatever you *want* to believe you deserve. Seriously, for real, and right now! The mechanism for adopting the belief that you deserve to make an abundant living as a writer is to simply *make the decision to believe it.* Just like adopting a new belief, you can craft an affirmation and visualization that supports the fact that you deserve whatever it is that you want. If you need some help in this area, consider this: if you don't deserve it, then who the heck does? The word desire literally means "of the stars," or "of the father." If you're a religious person, you'll get the reference right away. Either way, I believe what you desire desires you. And if you desire it, then you deserve it. End of discussion. Well, sort of.

The final step is to commit 100 percent to making money, an abundance of money, as a writer. Now you might be thinking, *Of course I'm committed 100 percent, Honorée, what do you mean?*

It is entirely possible that the idea of making an abundance of money as a writer sounds fantastic to you. So much so that you have worked through the process of thinking differently, creating a new belief, and even increasing your deserve-ability. But I have found that a lot of people commit to things, *sort of.* Just like we discussed in Chapter 1, there's a big difference between being *interested* and being *committed.* Which are you?

Don't be like the people who commit only to the extent that things work out. It wouldn't be right to commit only when things are going great. Especially if somewhere in the back of your mind you are holding onto the idea that, *If this doesn't work out, I can do that.* In other words, if you're working in a job you hate to pay the bills, you may think, *I'll give this making money as a writer thing a try, but if it doesn't work out, I always have ditch digging to fall back on* (or whatever it is you're doing to make money right now).

Now, I'm not suggesting that you throw caution to the wind, write your resignation letter, pack up all your belongings in a box, and head home to write your novel right now. I *am* suggesting that since you have made it this far and you're still reading, you really want to make a full-time living as a writer. Am I correct? (I thought so.) That means you need to make the commitment to making *full-time prosperous writer* your reality, and change not only your beliefs, but also your actions in order to make that happen. And, you need to pledge to stay committed to the process for as long as it takes.

GIVE YOURSELF PERMISSION TO MAKE MONEY AS A WRITER

If you made it this far, you are finally and fully ready to give yourself permission to make *real* money as a writer. The kind of money that allows you to abundantly support yourself, your family, any furry children you might have, and cover all of your life's responsibilities … with some left over for good measure. In addition to that, you'll want to indulge the artistic side of your inner writer and participate in extracurricular activities that feed and nurture your soul. As luck would have it, these activities tend to cost money.

Giving yourself permission to make money as a writer is simple and easy. Did you just get excited? I got excited writing that, for sure! Remember when I was asking about your commitment? As I said, I find that some people are more *interested* than committed. It's a distinction with a clear difference: when you're interested in something, you can easily become disinterested in it. In fact, at the slightest noise, distraction, new Facebook post by a friend, or season finale of your favorite show (not to mention challenge or problem), you can be thrown off course … never to return. However, when you are committed, getting the result you want is not a matter of if, it is a matter of *when*.

And, guess what? You don't need anyone's permission to make money as a writer. You don't need a doctor's note, your parents' signature, or any kind of legal document. You can just decide. So, while we're still rolling around here in chapter 2, will you decide?

Let me know when you're ready; I'll wait.

Oh good—you're still here! I'm so glad you are. I assume then that not only have you decided to eradicate any belief standing in your way of making money as a writer, but you've also given yourself full permission to do so. That's pretty exciting! Are you excited!? I am! Grab your prosperity journal, do your homework below, and then turn the page … it's about to get exciting up in here.

Homework:

Pull out your prosperity journal, identify an old "truth" or belief and create a new one using these steps as your guide:

1. Identify an old "truth."
2. How do you feel when you think its true?
3. Is it really the truth? (Hint: NO.)
4. Why is it false?
5. How do you feel now that you realize it's false?
6. What could your new truth be? Write it out, and start to live it.

3

YOUR JOURNEY TO BECOMING A PROSPEROUS WRITER

B y now you have identified at least one limiting belief. If you haven't truly adopted a new, empowering belief, you have at least begun the process of collapsing the old one. I don't know about you, but once I realized I had the power to choose what I believed, and ultimately my results, I was really, *really* excited.

I know that, of all the things I can share with you, the most important one is that you are the driver and decider of your life. You, and only you, ultimately determine your life, your results, and whether or not you become truly successful as a writer.

To make measurable progress on your journey to becoming a prosperous writer, you have to identify where you are right now. I call that starting point your Point A.. Abundant, prosperous writer status is where you're headed, and we call that Point B.

Even before you identify your Point A, it is important for us to take a moment to discuss *who* to take with you on your journey and *whom* you should leave at home. As we have discussed, it is a widely accepted societal belief that artists are poor and struggling. It wouldn't be surprising if you have a number of people in your life who, up until this point, believed that right along with you. It's even less surprising that these same people may be somewhat resistant to the idea of your expanding your consciousness so that you can expand what's in your wallet.

I don't want to spend a ton of time on this topic, but I believe it bears a quick mention. It is important that you invite on your journey only those who are 100 percent supportive. It is hard enough to transition our thinking; change, alter, and expand our beliefs; and get comfortable with a new level of abundance! We don't need to add the difficulty of justifying our thoughts, words, and actions to someone who is resistant to our new and exciting adventure. If they don't get it, they don't get it, and no amount of convincing on your part (other than those eventual checks) is going to do the trick.

A quick acid test can help you pick out these non-supporters. You'll notice that, when you share your goals, aspirations, and desired outcome with any person, they may say: "That's brilliant!" Or, they might say, "Well, honey, don't get your hopes up. Trying to make money as a writer is a poor man's errand." I'm sure you can decide which one is *acidic* to your new beliefs. I want to believe that everyone in your life has pure intentions and your best interests at heart, as I'm sure you do as well. So, we're going to assume any naysayers are doing their naysaying in an attempt to try to protect you from getting your soul crushed. However, some people like us just the way we are, and they are just fine with the struggle, even though they would deny that to their death. These folks wouldn't want you to make so much money that they felt uncomfortable with your abundance (or the fact that they've failed to go after their own dreams and you are a living, breathing example of that). Let me reiterate here—most of the time naysayers are doing the best they can and have no nefarious intentions. Nonetheless, the outcome is the same—they speak what they think is the truth, and you're left feeling awful. Not good.

You have two choices: you can share your new intentions of greater riches with everyone, or you can use your super powers of deduction and share your intended outcomes only with those folks you know will support you. If you share your new intentions with everyone, let's hope they fall in behind you, supporting you all the way. And for the folks you know will support you, we'd like them to follow us all the way to the bestseller list and bank!

Either way, you've picked up this book for a reason, and it is time to get you officially started! Are you ready?

LET THE GAMES BEGIN

I think it's important to establish some ground rules around becoming a prosperous writer. Money can be a very emotional and serious subject, and I understand that. But as a writer, you are an artist. And isn't being an artist fun? Or, more to the point, isn't it supposed to be? I take my writing, and my money, very seriously. But, I have one general life rule: if it isn't fun, I don't do it.

To that end, I want to be clear that we are going to make the process of becoming a prosperous writer fun. It will be full of enjoyable activities, such as: writing, cashing checks, getting excited about various projects, making delicious writer friends, and noticing lots of cool abundance all around us. You'll be just like the writers you admire—doesn't that sound great? In order to become one of them, you must start to think, say, and do what they do. Starting with …

PROSPEROUS WRITERS KEEP PERSPECTIVE

Every person who has accumulated significant wealth as a writer was once an aspiring writer. Joanna Penn, of The Creative Penn, contributes, "Every person who has gotten 'there' once started 'here,' and once you get 'there,' then you identify a new 'there.'" Prosperous writers are always revising and expanding their goals and outcomes. For right now (this will be in your homework at the end of the chapter), you will define where "there" is for you today. Trust me when I say that someday you will look back and be amazed at how far you've come! With the goal to become a self-sustaining, prosperous author, it is easy to be forward focused and neglect to see any progress that's been made up to this point. Do yourself, and your sanity, a huge favor and make note of your progress thus far. Write down in your prosperity journal where you started. It could be writing stories in third grade, or perhaps you have 17 years of freelance experience. Either way, you're a writer, and you have some things to show for it. You won't see your growth unless you take a moment to truly acknowledge it. This exercise doesn't need to take more than five minutes or so, but it is always helpful to take a moment to notice how far we've come and give ourselves a pat on the back.

PROSPEROUS WRITERS HAVE AWESOME BELIEFS

You may think I'm talking an awful lot about beliefs in this book, and you would be right because your beliefs are what drive you (or don't drive you) and you've got to master them. As I've mentioned, there are two ways to change a belief. The one we can most effectively use, the one that will make a difference for you sooner rather than later, is repetition. Did you know that an affirmation is anything you say to yourself over and over? There's no qualifier, meaning it doesn't *have* to be positive (in fact, many affirmations could be classified as negative!). When you say to yourself over and over something like "I don't have the time to write," or "Making money as a writer is a fool's errand," those are affirmations. That's right, even things that aren't positive are affirmations when you say them to yourself over and over again. Surely by now you recognize you don't want to affirm something you don't actually want to be your truth! Whatever you tell your subconscious mind is taken as a directive, and it does everything it can to prove you right. Let's make sure what you are repeating and telling your subconscious mind is working for you and on your behalf.

Here is one of my favorite affirmations of all time, and as it became my belief, it became my reality: "I turn the great energy of my thinking upon ideas of plenty, and I have plenty, regardless of what people about me are saying or doing."

I particularly love this affirmation for you right now because it will reinforce the fact that you retain control over your income and prosperity as a writer, regardless of what anyone is telling you. I still have the original 5 x 7 note card on which I wrote that affirmation twenty years ago. It lives on the side of my refrigerator, and I see it and say it aloud every morning. In the morning I have my protein shake and vitamins and say this affirmation as a part of my routine. I use it to continually reinforce my belief that the great energy of my thinking is what creates my results—not the economy, not tradition, and certainly not an age-old maxim.

PROSPEROUS WRITERS PRESUME SUCCESS

Prosperous writers presume their own success. I know for a fact you must presume yours. You must presume it today, even if your Point A seems like a million miles from your destination. Try this: when someone asks you what you do, say, "I am a writer." The next sentence for me is, "I write nonfiction for professionals who want to be more effective, efficient, have more time, and make more money." You'll want to craft your own sentence such as, "I am a writer! I write fictional mysteries for readers who want fast-paced, thrilling entertainment."

Finally, you'll take that second sentence, and add five key important words to the beginning of it: "I earn an abundant living writing _____ for _____ who want _____." For example, mine now looks like: "I earn an abundant living writing nonfiction for professionals who want to be more effective, efficient, have more time, and make more money."

Why is it important to take the time to design these three sentences, memorize them, and say them over, and over, and over? Because, my friend, you are programming your subconscious mind. Your belief systems must be tackled first. We haven't yet talked about plans, but when we do, I'm sure you will be inspired to create one. You can come up with the best plan in the world, but if your beliefs don't support it, in the end you won't take any action. Your beliefs will literally stop you before you ever really get a chance to get started, and that would be tragic.

Now, we can put all of these sentences together:

"I am a writer. I write nonfiction for professionals who want to be more effective, efficient, have more time, and make more money. I earn an abundant living writing nonfiction for professionals who want to be more effective, efficient, have more time, and make more money."

As your limiting beliefs pop up in the future, do the exercise from Chapter 2 to collapse each belief, and then write the three sentences above for as many beliefs as you need. There is no limit to the number of positive words you can design and use to program your mind for success. Say these affirmations at least twice a day. I'd suggest saying them more often if you notice negative emotions or emotional resistance showing up for you. An affirmation, such as the one I've written for myself above, is a great antidote to the fear of failure (or fear of anything else for that matter).

Prosperous Writers Have Unwavering Faith, Take Consistent Action & Exercise Patience

Unwavering faith, consistent action, and a ton of patience—these three characteristics make up a very powerful triangle. This trifecta of awesomeness, if you will, creates an environment of success for writers as well as aspiring writers. Let me break them down for you one by one so you can integrate them into your thought processes as well.

Let's start with unwavering faith. This is a big one, especially in the face of *I'm not yet making a living from my writing, My spouse isn't supportive*, or, frankly, any number of discouragements you might be facing. Unwavering faith is a belief you develop in yourself and your vision that you know will get the results you want if you hang in there long enough (regardless of the results you're seeing today).

Consistent action is the next point of the triangle and is a mighty important factor in your success. Taking daily action on the plans you've created will ultimately yield the results you want. Think about this: if you write 1,000 words per day, at the end of the year you'll have written 365,000 words. By anyone's account, that is a great year! The byproduct of all of those words is anywhere from three to twelve books, or countless articles, depending upon whether you write fiction, nonfiction, and in what genre you focus. Pretty cool, right?

Finally, patience is your new best friend. The more patient you are (in combination with your faith and action), the better off you will be from a mental and spiritual perspective. If you can play the long game, all a part of building a strong "patience muscle," you will enjoy the journey even more.

There are two separate and distinct action items for you to use to help you adopt the practices of unwavering faith, consistent action, and patience. The first is a five-step process you can do, which will take anywhere from five to twenty minutes a day. You can do each practice for one minute, or you can take up to four minutes per practice.

The first practice is silence. During your time of silence, you will just *be silent*. Close your eyes, take a deep breath, and just be in this moment. Give your mind a chance to clear out and reboot. If you create an environment for your mind to settle down, then it will. Enjoy the silence. Allow the tension in your entire body to disappear. A calm mind leads to a calm body.

During the next minute, think of what you can do to show active appreciation for anything and everything you are grateful for in your life right now. This isn't about just being grateful, although gratitude is certainly a fantastic practice. I believe showing your gratitude, otherwise known as active appreciation, is next-level goodness. Think of something you are grateful for and think of what you can do to *show* your gratitude for it.

The next practice is visualization, but this is not your ordinary, garden-variety visualization. This is a *what if?* visualization that will change the course of your future! I know, I get excited when I talk about this stuff … The most recent exercise you did was stringing three sentences together that represent what you want your writer life to look like. I would imagine you want that future vision to show up and be your reality, like posthaste (me, too!). To kick off the *what if* visualization, you can use the example below.

What if I was paid millions of dollars to write nonfiction for professionals who want to be more effective, efficient, have more time, and make more money? How fun would that be? Visualize the end result as real, and see yourself having all of the fun you can imagine (or whatever your end result is going to bring for you). Spending between one and four minutes in a creative place of pretend, while creating a mental movie of what you desire, will hasten its coming to you. Yup, that's right—you get to sit and visualize what you want your future to look like, and because you are doing that, you get to have that future faster. Pretty amazing, I'd say!

After you finish your visualization, spend a moment just allowing what you have been visualizing to come to you. You literally don't have to do anything; you must just sit there and allow. Start to breathe normally again. If, as in my case, you're breathing rate increases as you imagine your vision in full Technicolor and surround-sound, remember to relax and let it happen. Allow all of the good you're expecting come to you, and create a space for it in your mind, body, and spirit. I believe the majority of our results come from who we are be-ing, not always what we are do-ing.

Finally, the time has come to turn up your vibration. I would like you to imagine you have a dial in the center of your chest, and it is currently set on the number one. You can visualize turning up the dial, or you can act as if you are actually turning up a dial. Either one will work just fine. For the next minute (or four minutes) take yourself from number one to number two, three, four, and finally to number five. Number five on the dial is you, fired up and excited about your amazing future! Imagine yourself making a living, an abundant living, out those three previously created sentences as though they are your real-life reality right now. As if you opened your eyes to that reality right now, today. That is your number five, or level five, vibration.

I love how I feel at a level five vibration. I feel unstoppable, confident, and as though the words will just flow from the tips of my fingers. When I feel like I'm at my best, I also feel like life is just rolling along in the most perfect way possible. I'm getting the results I want, and making the progress I want to make ... Life is good.

But what about when life isn't so good? What about the times you come up against challenges that seem to stop you in your tracks? In chapter 6, I discuss overcoming challenges and actually seeing them as opportunities in disguise, including some no-nonsense strategies you can use when the going gets tough. But, there is one thing you can start doing right now that will impact all of your situations in a positive way, whether those situations are actually positive or not so much.

EVERYTHING IS TRULY A BLESSING

You can begin to practice one of the basic strategies for happy living that also happens to be a practice of prosperous writers. This strategy is actually common, and not so common. This strategy is an ancient secret for happy living, and it is the act of blessing. As a common practice, most of us have heard the terms blessing, bless you, or even let's say a blessing over a meal. Seldom do we realize we have the power to experience health, harmony, and prosperity through using the practice of blessing over everything in our lives, up to, and including, our writing.

I know that the act of blessing anything carries with it great power. The dictionary explains why there is dynamic power for good in the simple art of blessing. To bless means, "to make holy or whole by spoken words." To bless means to, "ask divine favor for some situation or condition." Blessing means, "to wish a person or situation well." To bless even means, "to make happy or prosperous." And finally, to bless means to, "gladden, glorify, and praise."

We might simply say that to bless means to "bring forth good in a situation, condition, or person," whether it seems like there's any good to be brought forth or not. It may seem as though having a prosperous writing career isn't a reality you can create, but I beg to differ. That is why I'm sharing with you this supercool and unbelievably amazing, effective tactic for taking even the most bleak situation and not just finding the good in it, but using your power to create good from it. Blessing a situation means you're not judging it according to its current appearance—you're using the power you have within you to behold the good and thereby bring it forth in a condition or person ... and in your writing.

Think of it this way: how often have you condemned, criticized, or cursed a situation? You may not have realized you used your power to perhaps bring forth more unhappy and undesired problems or experiences. If you had dared to take the opposite view, and blessed the situation, you would have activated the omnipresent good within it and witnessed a happy result. The great news is you can start to do that at any moment—like this one.

The ability you have to write is your blessing to use, and you will, in fact, find that the more you use your talent and ability to write (or any talent or ability you have), the happier you will be. I want you to consider using your power of blessing in the face of challenges, frustrations, and situations that cause you to feel any one of a number of negative emotions, especially in your your writing career.

There is a three-step process you will find helpful for blessing any situation:

1. Get quiet.
2. Stop negatively talking or complaining to anyone about the situation.
3. Bless the situation.

Simple, right? The students in the Prosperity for Writers course loved the idea of blessing challenging situations. Leslie shared that she felt like it gave her power, where before she had felt powerless. Your job is to go within yourself; get rid of any critical, cynical, and unpleasant attitudes; start praising every situation for its good points rather than condemning it for its bad points; start treating the situation as though it does not exist; and to resume normal activities as though there is no challenge at all. When well-meaning relatives and friends ask for the latest news on the subject (mostly for their own private entertainment), don't say anything negative. It may be a bit of a challenge for you to stop talking about how frustrating a situation is, particularly if that situation is a lack of progress in your pursuit of prosperity. However, as you begin to bless your situation daily, you will find that the situation will right itself—almost as if by magic.

Begin now to bless every situation in your life as good. When you bless anything, you are calling forth the good within it, and you will be pleasantly surprised at all of the good you find in these "negative" situations and the good that comes through them. When I say every situation, I do mean *every* situation: bless your money, problems, food, current job, books you've published and the ones you're still writing … and any and everything else in between. You must also be sure to bless anything, or anyone, that is currently causing you trouble. If you are experiencing lack, such as a lack of words or lack of money, why not take a few seconds to throw in a blessing! I mean, it's free, and you can turn any situation around as quick as a wink … even an empty bank account into a full one or a manuscript lacking in words into one overflowing with an abundance of words! I promise you can literally bless anything into something good.

Of course, I think it is important to point out there are a few things it would be best not to do. You would be well served to avoid being stressed, anxious, or worried. I know, I know. You've been stressed, anxious and worried for a long time. You are amazing at it! How about trying something new? Just for the duration of this book, (and the time it takes you to complete your homework) take off your stressed/anxious/worried hat, and put on your I-expect-something-amazing-to-happen hat instead. Because I'm not a purely motivation-without-practical-practices kind of gal, I'm going to share with you exactly how to do that. Allow me to introduce you to your new friend, the "BOLO."

BOLO: Be on the Lookout!

I am a big believer in starting things right away. As a matter of fact, I believe some people have a now setting or a later setting. I definitely have the now setting, which means when it's time to start doing something, the time is usually right now.

We are going to start with your prosperity transformation right now. I'm sure you have watched one of the thousands of police dramas on television. Maybe you are the author of police dramas, or crime dramas, or you want to be, so the term BOLO is not unfamiliar. Usually, after a crime, a witness will describe the fleeing suspect. The detective will then say, "Let's put out a BOLO on the suspect." BOLO is an acronym for "be on the lookout" for.

I don't use BOLO in the traditional pursuit-of-crime sense. I've adopted the BOLO term for use on my journey to becoming rich. When I had the Prosperity for Writers course, the first assignment was to BOLO, and yours is too. Let me explain. If you want to become prosperous, in any way, the first step is to notice all of the abundance that surrounds you. You might see an abundance of rain, flowers, gold Volkswagens, or red doors.

There is abundance surrounding us every day in so many ways. But, if haven't been specifically looking for abundance, you probably haven't noticed abundance. Makes sense, right? Pull out your prosperity journal and write down everything you can see an abundance of in your world. From my balcony, I can see more cars, trees, and even light poles than I can count. I live in central Texas, and this year we have had an abundance of rain. Because I'm on the lookout for abundance, I see abundance everywhere. Right now I'm on a packed plane—I see an abundance of people!

What you want is an abundance of money, correct? Okay then, here's what I want you to look for: people you know, and people you don't, making their living (i.e., an abundance of money) from writing. Look for, and make note of, all of the places you make money from writing. My books are published everywhere a self-published author can publish their books. That means I receive money from multiple sources from the sales of my books every single month. In some instances, I receive money weekly (and sometimes daily).

Now, take a few minutes to notice the similarities between you and the people you've noted who are making money from their writing. Let me remind you that there are no special writers, only people who are a bit further along the path than you are and who are making money from their writing. Some make more, some make less. Your job is to BOLO—be on the lookout for these prosperous writers.

In the next chapter, I'm going to give you more tools, action steps, and, yes, more homework. In fact, at the end of every chapter, I'm going to share action items that will serve you on your journey to becoming a full-fledged, prosperous, moneymaking writing machine. Sound good?

Note: As a coach, I almost always give action items to my clients. All of these action items mean something—similar to the action "wax on, wax off" from *The Karate Kid*. It might not always seem like there's a method to my madness, but I assure you there is. Set aside any hesitations you might have or any resistance you might be feeling, and at least give 'em a try. You truly don't have anything to lose, and everything to gain.

Note: you can always stop using them and go back to business as usual anytime. But, what have you got to lose? I'm just sayin'.

HOMEWORK:

1. What beliefs have you shifted?

2. How do these shifts make you feel?

3. What is everything you're grateful for? Make sure to put in something where you can be actively appreciative. Complete the circle by showing gratitude for something awesome that's happened for you.

4. BOLOing—you're looking for evidence of abundance in the world, and evidence of writers who make an abundance of money.

5. Is there something else holding you back? If so, eradicate the belief, and if you hit another ceiling, eradicate again. Rinse and repeat.

6. Here are your three sentences to use as affirmations (which you will want to repeat daily):

   - I am a writer.

   - I write _____ for _____ who want _____. (Example: I write nonfiction for professionals who want to make more money in less time.)

   - I make an abundant living writing _____ for _____ who want _____. (Example: I make an abundant living writing nonfiction for professionals who want to make more money in less time.)

7. Say these sentences out loud whenever your lizard brain (a.k.a. monkey mind) starts to make noise. Say them while you're in the shower, car, and making dinner—all day, every day, until you own them, and they own you.

4

GET FAME FOR PROSPERITY

S uccessful writers don't become successful overnight, and their success is not happenstance. To help you get from where you are to where you want to be as quickly as possible, I'm going to share with you the main aspects of prosperous writers. Then, I'll show you how you can adopt them for yourself. For this purpose, I'm going to use the acronym "FAME." But this fame isn't what you might think—it's not necessarily about becoming famous, although that might end up happening for you. Each of the letters in FAME stand for an important aspect, or aspects, prosperous writers use to grow their writing businesses and earn more income.

The first "F" in FAME is *friends*. In order to be a prosperous writer, it's helpful to have lots of friends, and not just close, personal friends (although we all need those). The friends I'm referring to are the friends and connections you collect as you build your platform. These include your total Facebook connections, Twitter and Instagram followers, LinkedIn connections as well as your writer friends.

My friend, Deborah Coonts, author of the *Lucky O'Toole* series (a fun, sexy, murder mystery series set in Las Vegas), has many friends who write in her genre as well as some of us who write thrillers, romance, and even nonfiction. She's met those friends all along her writer journey, including meeting them at conferences and writer's events. I, myself, have had a great time connecting with fellow writers. These friends in particular have made suggestions, provided advice, shared tips and tools as well as just given some general (much needed and appreciated) encouragement along the way. I've also corresponded and connected with hundreds of my readers. I love hearing from them, and it seems as though they feel the same when they hear from me. Get as connected as you can to as many friends as you can because being a writer can sometimes be rather lonely. After all, most of our words are written in isolation. But when we close the lid on our laptops, it's great to be able to connect with people who know, like, and understand us. You will find that the successful writers you admire tend to know and support each other. As you proceed in your transformation, you'll want to connect with them as well as with many others.

The second "F" in FAME is *focus*. Without a doubt, successful and prosperous writers get focused and stay focused. Overall, their most intense focus may be solely on their desired outcome. That means they also have a clear vision they are focused on, whatever that happens to be. One of your areas of genius is writing, and you have determined you are going to go to work and earn money in this unique area of genius. To do so, you will have to develop the ability to focus. If your focus muscle is weak, this will be an area of focus for you (pun intended). In other words, as you are developing the skill of your craft, you'll need to concentrate on creating your focus skills. Define your outcome, and focus solely on this outcome. We will talk about plans in this book, but let me say this right now: you won't create or execute a plan if you don't believe you can make your intended results happen.

The first "A" in FAME is *ass in seat*, which, in case you were wondering, is the technical term. Successful, prosperous writers sit down and write the words they need to write. These words help build the work product they *must* create in order to make the money they want to make. Most writers figure out what time of day works best for them to write. I, myself, am able to write better and faster in the early morning hours. If by chance I'm unable to write until later in the day, I find the words don't come as quickly or easily as they do earlier in the day. I have engineered circumstances and my schedule so that I am able to get at least 20 – 60 minutes of writing first thing in the morning. You will want to determine what time of day works best for you and add a recurring appointment to your daily calendar. Then, all you have to do is what your calendar tells you to do. I know, it's as simple as it sounds.

As you define your goals, you will define your production plan. And as you are doing that, there are a few questions to ask yourself:

- *If you weren't resistant and/or afraid to write and create to your heart's content, what would you write and create?*

- *If you did have a picture of yourself sitting in writing, where would you write?*

- *When would you write?*

- *What does being a successful, prosperous writer look like to you?*

Don't be shocked that I'm going to recommend you answer all of these questions. You'll need to answer them in writing, in your prosperity journal. You can bet the writers you admire have answered these questions, in writing, for themselves. It would behoove you to take the time to get very clear about what you want and then define *when* and *what* you need to do to make it happen—including writing all those words!

The second "A" in FAME is *attitude*. Successful people, specifically successful writers, have an unwavering belief in themselves. You must, and I mean *must*, adopt an attitude that serves you in the best and most positive way. Here are some more things to define in your prosperity journal: what beliefs, or attitudes, do you need to adopt?

If you need additional help in this area, I suggest you read the book *Psycho-Cybernetics* by Maxwell Maltz. Or, you can get the audio program, of the same name, done by Dan Kennedy. Dan inspired me when I listened to his program long before I thought of writing my first book. Some people have writers block, but in the *Psycho Cybernetics* audio program, Dan shared that he had to write the equivalent of 200,000 words (equaling at least two very large books) each month, along with doing a significant amount of other writing projects. In other words, no time for writer's block! He shared that he had a belief that whenever he had the time to sit down to write, the words flowed effortlessly from his fingertips, *no matter what*.

If you are someone who believes you can only write when you are facing East at sunset on a Tuesday while listening to Mozart, you might want to adopt a new, more empowering belief. I chose to take on Dan's belief that when I sit down to write, the words flow effortlessly from my fingertips ... *so they do*. Whatever belief you define that serves you at the highest level, write it on a sticky note, or 3 x 5 card, and put the card where you will see it all day every day. Even when you're not focused on it, you will have the benefit of your subconscious mind taking note of this belief, which will immediately or eventually turn into reality for you. Take a few moments right now and decide what your new belief is about writing, and also identify the upgrades you need to make in your attitude.

Another aspect of *attitude* is to take ownership and stewardship over your writing and your writing career. The buck stops with you. You are no longer a victim of chance or circumstances. You are a victor choosing to create your desired results. I personally don't like things to be hard. I want to do whatever is necessary for me to have an easier path, a faster way, and, without question, a positive attitude in which I take ownership and stewardship as an accelerator in my own success.

You'll also need to be incredibly flexible—you're going to keep trying things until something works. Keep seeking until you find the thing, or things, that work for you and allow you to produce quality work at an amazing pace. Just know that at some point you're going to turn the corner, and the work and money will start flowing freely. Eventually you will gain the momentum you want and start to see the positive results stacking up.

The final "A" in FAME is *authority*. Prosperous writers have an authority only an author can have: a platform, also known as readers, friends, and other important connections. You have to believe there are people who want to read what you're writing. And, just as I mentioned above with developing friends, you have to connect with those people. Jay Abraham, marketing genius and major platform generator, says, "Fall in love with your customer, not your product." Let's change that to, "Fall in love with your reader, not your books." Authors have authority, and it's time for you to develop yours. Wherever you are on that path, you can find inspiration on how to do it faster and easier in books like *Your First 1000 Copies* by Tim Grahl.

The first "M" in FAME is *money consciousness*. Prosperous writers believe, think, talk, and act like it is okay (like amazingly okay) for them to make money from their writing. Being prosperous is good, and receiving money is *good*. Money coming to you (from multiple sources) on a continuous basis from your writing is good! You must believe you are doing something of value. In addition to believe, you must desire to be paid for this value you're producing. Period. Got it? Maybe you don't, and that's the entire reason you're reading this book. Then, my friends, you must take a hard look at your money consciousness and figure out if it needs expanding. If you are leaning more toward *lack of limitation* than *prosperous and abundant*, do yourself (and your eventual readers) a favor and get to the place where you are comfortable with money coming to you from your writing—believe that this really is a good thing. I believe that it is, for myself and for you, or frankly I wouldn't have taken the time to write this book. There isn't a single successful writer I interviewed for this book, or that I know personally, who makes any apology for being prosperous. Neither should you!

The second "M" in FAME is *mental state.* Our minds are goal-seeking mechanisms. For the duration of this book, and hopefully forever, you will be BOLO-ing. You will be on the lookout not only for abundance, but also for more of anything and everything you want. BOLO-ing turns on the reticular activating system—the part of your brain that notices what you're looking for. If you drive a blue Toyota sedan, you will notice every other blue Toyota sedan that is the same make, model, and year as yours. Chances are, you're going to notice the exact make, model, and year of your spouse's car as well. You can use this ability (noticing) to your highest advantage by directing your brain to look for instances of abundance: writers who are making enough money to live on their writing, every single time you receive money for your writing, and anything else your heart desires. For instance, if you meet someone for coffee and he or she treats you to a cup of coffee, that's abundance. You didn't have to spend your own money on a cup of coffee. Be sure to notice and write down every instance of abundance you experience. Noticing will actually encourage other instances of abundance in your life.

Remember: people you admire who are successful are not special, or at least they are no more special than you are special. Successful, prosperous writers are people who have the beliefs that they are meant to be successful and earn money from their writing. That's really all there is to it. In their programming, they believe they deserve to make money from the writing, and so they do. If you see them as special, or even hate them, you are doing yourself a disservice. You can choose: I want to be like them or I resent them. Which one is going to be more effective in getting you more of what you want? You can resent J.K. Rowling for earning more than a billion dollars from her books, and everything else amazing that has happened to her because she wrote those books. But I can assure you, she isn't thinking or worrying herself about you and what you think; she's out shopping! Do yourself a huge service and admire what others have created. Emulate the tactics they have used that resonate with you, and duplicate their success for yourself.

The first "E" in FAME is *execute*. You will have to execute the plan or plans you create. Beliefs are important when creating plans because if you don't believe you can create the result you want, then you won't execute on your plan. Double circle and underline your new belief or beliefs, and then create a goal based on the new beliefs. This includes a plan to support that goal and the production schedule that supports reaching those goals. I absolutely believe in visualizing success, and I engage in visualization everyday. But, if all I ever did was visualize myself writing, instead of actually opening up my computer and writing, you wouldn't be holding this book in your hand. Visualization is good, but, practically speaking, and as I've said before, you truly have to write the words. Don't worry; you won't have to reinvent the wheel on this one. I have included a couple of plans for you to use in this book, and you'll find them in chapter 6.

The final "E" in FAME is *expectation*, specifically *positive expectation*. Some people live in perpetual negative expectation: *I'm afraid this or that is going to happen*, and because that's what they're transmitting out into the world, that's exactly what they're getting. You might know it as a self-fulfilling prophecy. If that's the case, let's get you turned around and fully engaged in a perpetual state of positive expectation—one where you are hopped up and excited about what's to come in your near and long-term future. Look at it this way: the best time to close a deal is right after you've closed a deal. You're still excited, so it's no surprise something else good comes along. Writing is no different. The best time to write your words is the day after you've written words. The more you write, the more you write. The more you make from your writing, the more you make from your writing. It's an end run around actually being a prosperous writer in today's world, and the way to get there is to put you mentally there first. Write down in your prosperity journal what you are positively expecting. But here's the trick: write it as though it just happened, or as though it happened last week, last month, or last year. Here's the start to your sentence: *"I am so happy and grateful now that…"* You could finish that sentence with, "I received royalties in excess of $3,000," or "I finished my book and I love watching my sales grow on KDP." The rest of the sentence is up to you. And by golly, you're a writer, so get positively expectant, creative, and write something that excites and inspires you!

> *"If you believe you can, or if you believe*
> *you can't, you're right."*
>
> –Henry Ford

Johnny B. Truant, co-host of the *Self-Publishing Podcast* and author of multiple fiction and nonfiction books repeated what many others have said, *"I get 30 percent of what I want, of the goals I set. I stay positive that each thing I try is going to work out. Some things don't, but I soldier on and ignore the nay-sayers."* Because he never knows what's going to hit, he just keeps going, and he never entertains the idea of giving up. *"There's a problem with our culture. I think there's a badge of honor from being a starving artist. If someone has never presented you with the idea you can prosper as a writer, based on what society has told us, you're probably going to think you always have to struggle. And, that's just not true."*

By now I hope you can see that becoming a prosperous writer is a combination of working smart and thinking right. I don't mean there's a wrong way to think. How you think is more aptly described as effective or ineffective. If you want to get the FAME of prosperous writers, you must follow their lead. By all accounts, they are effective thinkers and action takers. I think it's high time you became one, too!

Homework:

Answer the following questions:

1. If you weren't afraid to write and create to your heart's content, what would you write and create?

   - If you did have a picture of yourself sitting in writing, where would you write?
   - When would you write?
   - What does being a successful, prosperous writer look like to you?

2. Finish this sentence: I am so happy and grateful now that ...

3. Make a list of everything you're grateful for today.

5

WHAT'S YOUR MONEY STORY?

J ust like you have beliefs around money, you also have what I call your money story. Chances are your money story originated in childhood, which pretty much means you didn't have any control over creating it. But that doesn't mean it hasn't been the source of the overall direction of your prosperity consciousness, and therefore your actual prosperity, and your entire life thus far. *Because it has.* Of course it stands to reason that the money story that runs your life is also running your writing.

It took me a long time to realize I had a money story and that the beliefs that were the basic construct of that story were holding me back in major (and minor) ways.

MY MONEY STORY

It was either feast or famine in my house. Sometimes my parents had money, and sometimes they didn't—more often, they didn't. I believe this was because they never quite found peace with money. They never got to a place where they believed making an abundance of money was truly good.

When money was scarce, my mother used grocery money to buy extras and necessities for my brothers and me. When she bought non-food necessities with food money, the implication was clear: *You'd better appreciate this because you're literally taking food out of the mouths of the rest of the family.* In addition, both of my parents reiterated their beliefs to always "Buy the best quality of anything you can afford, and take excellent care of it." From that directive, I took two things: take good care of the quality item you are able to buy because you should take good care of anything you own. But you'd also better take care of what you buy because you may never, *ever* be able to buy another one.

You can see both the positive and negative sides of that belief, right? I always buy quality, and take great care of it. But for the longest time, I had this feeling in the back of my mind that if something happened to my prized possession I may never be able to get another one.

When I started doing my own prosperity work more than 20 years ago, I wish I had recognized the beliefs that were the basis of my money story, and how they were affecting me on a daily basis. Because I was bringing those unconscious beliefs and that story with me into my adult life, they literally drove my every behavior—especially my behavior around money. It took me a really long time to think of something as an item I was able to own and use (such as a computer or a sweater) and that when I had worn them out, or was even ready for a new one, I would have the resources at my disposal to simply get another one.

Once I recognized I had beliefs that weren't working for me, I decided to adopt some new ones. One of my current beliefs is: *I can always get more money.* I've also recognized that, while I can always get more money, I cannot get more time. I have expanded my consciousness about money and have simultaneously become much more protective of my time. Another belief is *"As money goes out, immediately double the money comes in."* I love this belief, and it comes in handy all the time. Whether I'm dying for a drink at Starbucks, or writing a check for a brand-new car, I'm silently affirming that double the money is coming back to me, and in pretty short order. While I've been able to temper my negative beliefs about money, I'm still rather impatient and love instant gratification. So, I for sure want double the money to come back within a couple of days, if not a couple of hours.

You can adopt these two beliefs for yourself if you'd like, and in addition, choose ones that resonate with you. Once you start to notice where your beliefs are holding you back and you decide to BOLO while you're engaging in some new ones, you'll find inspiration from Leslie Watts, who was a participant in the Prosperity for Writers course. She sent me the following email a week after the first class:

QUICK CHECK-IN!

I've been BOLO-ing, and I've had the experience all week of things falling into place—finding lost items, having enough time (though I was nervous about it), people showing up just when I need them, and a big chunk of money to pay for our remodel sitting in the bank in plenty of time. I also am noticing where the negative beliefs are surfacing and countering them. The affirmation you shared has helped so much. I've been catching myself before I attach to someone else's thoughts about plenty. What a relief!

I won't lie to you. It's been a challenging few days in many ways, but the tools you've shared have helped on the abundance and prosperity front. For sure. :)

Can't wait for class tomorrow!

Thanks for everything!

Leslie

In case you missed it, the affirmation is: "I turn the great energy of my thinking upon ideas of plenty, and I have plenty, regardless of what people about me are saying or doing."

YOUR ACTIONS AND REACTIONS ARE VISCERAL, BUT ...

Keep in mind that the money story that lives within you causes your actions and reactions to be automatic—almost beyond your control—but not quite! These visceral reactions spring up from the deep and subconscious wells of your mind and body, as if by magic. But they surely don't feel like magic, at least they didn't and don't to me. So, if by chance reading this book has caused you to pull out a hammer and start beating yourself over the head with it (as some have been known to do), I say, "Put the hammer down."

Sadly, we are not taught to be the captain of our beliefs. Rather, they are instilled and installed unbeknownst to us, some of them even before we can speak. You may have done prosperity work before, or this may be your first rodeo. In either case, with awareness comes power. You now have the power to identify, eradicate, change, and/or reverse beliefs. You will discover them based upon the automatic reactions you see yourself having, and the visceral reactions you find yourself experiencing—sometimes at the most inopportune moment.

When you notice yourself acting or reacting in a way you know doesn't serve you, jot down what belief you're holding that is driving your behavior. If you're not able to do the work to collapse that belief and identify a new one right then, put a date on your calendar to do that work.

I decided that I wanted my money story to be, *Not only do I always have an abundance of money, there's always more coming.* Let's face it, there's plenty of money in the world, and you alone cannot spend all of that money (although I'd love to give that a try!). Just as you have to rewrite your money story, you will need to identify beliefs that fit into, and are the basis of, that new story. In order to do that, you'll want to identify your current money story and your beliefs. This is a process of noticing and observing. It certainly isn't the time to be hard on yourself or beat yourself up. Your money story has most likely both served you and worked against you, just as mine had. Recognize it for what it is, what it isn't, how it has served you up to this point, and how it is a disservice to you. What keeps showing up for you? How is that working for you?

As I mentioned, I have always purchased top-quality items, the very best I could afford, and I have taken really good care of them. Once I got clear that a thing is just a *thing* and I can always get another one, I was in pretty good shape—because the other side of the belief really served me and still does.

You will most likely find that you can take the best of your beliefs and the best of your money story and use them to your advantage. Then you can take anything that is a disservice to you and rewrite it to your liking. After all, you are a writer, right?

IDENTIFY YOUR CURRENT MONEY STORY

Once again, it's time for your prosperity journal. If you are like the students in the Prosperity for Writers course, your mind is spinning right about now and searching for how your money story has informed and influenced your life up to this point. Write down what you notice, think of, and what occurs to you. Here are some thoughts to help you identify your story:

- How do you feel when it is time to spend a large amount of money?

- How do you react when you find out you have an unexpected expense, like a large car repair?

- Do you hoard money? Why?

- Do you consider yourself generous or stingy?

- How did you observe your parents or caregivers behave around money? How has that impacted, affected, or influenced the way you behave with and around money?

Once you make note of your money story and how it has impacted you over the course of your life, you will be able to identify how it has served you—as well as all of your resulting beliefs. You'll additionally become aware of the ways they have been a disservice to you.

IDENTIFY YOUR NEW MONEY STORY

Your imaginative center, the part of your brain that is creative and allows you to literally make things up, is part of your gift. You've been given the gift to imagine anything you want to imagine. As a writer, you can craft a wonderful story that's all about you living as a happy, prosperous writer.

Up to this point, you may have been using your gift of imagination to torture and terrorize yourself. In other words, what you've been picturing in your mind around making money as a writer may have been: *"I literally can not see myself prosperous as a writer."* And that's okay, but you are probably realizing right about now, if you haven't already, that picturing yourself as a failure is ineffective.

Hey, guess what? You are a writer, and it's time to write a new money story.

I'm sure you have an idea of what you would like your life to be like as a prosperous writer. I sure do! Five years ago when I crafted my 2015 vision, I got excited about what life would be like for me, my family, and the income I would be producing from my writing. I can say that today, at the close of those five years, it went by really fast! I can also say that those five years were full of challenges, interesting events, and magical opportunities. The target date for my five-year vision is September 23, 2015, just a month and five days after the publication of this book (and also known as my birthday). I can honestly say that, in the process of turning my vision into reality, it both looks everything and nothing like I had in mind. Most of the money I am earning from my writing comes from sources I had no knowledge of five years ago. I receive monthly income from projects that weren't even ideas, and from connections I didn't even have five years ago. But the end result is that I am earning an abundant income from my writing, and that was my original vision.

As you are crafting your five-year, one-year, or even six-month vision to earn money as a writer, I encourage you to focus solely on the outcome. In other words, don't get hung up on the mechanisms. Don't try to predict specifically where the income is going to come from. Only predict that you are going to write the words and the money is going to come. The money is going to flow into your life on a continuous basis, at increasing amounts, and from multiple sources for your own use. Personally, I'm not concerned with whether the money shows up in a box on my doorstep; a direct deposit from Amazon, Barnes & Noble, or Smashwords; or from someone who sees me speak and hands me 20 bucks cash in exchange for one of my books.

Right in line with your vision is your money story and the beliefs that support that money story. It will be fun for you to set aside the time to carefully craft the money story and beliefs that put a broad smile on your face and a spring in your step. If you write something like, "I earn $20,000 per month from my books and other writing," ask yourself, *What do I need to believe in order for that to happen?* A belief along the lines of, *Every time I release a new book, my followers can't wait to read it!* would be helpful. Additionally, you'll want to throw in a belief about your income increasing every month—if that's something you'd like (of course it is!). I have heard authors on podcasts talk about how they prepare for down months, or months where their income fluctuates greatly from the month before. I myself am not a fan of fluctuations, so I make sure to believe my income increases month over month.

Regardless of the beliefs that you decide to change or adopt, there's a fun game you can play. As I spend money, I expect double that amount of money to come to me. I expect money to come back to me whenever I pay a bill, pick up a check, buy a cup of coffee, or purchase anything and everything. I'm always thinking to myself, *I wonder where the money is going to come from to replace* this *money.*

THE PROSPERITY FOR WRITERS COURSE STUDENTS SAY ...

LESLIE WATTS:

Through the course and what you've shared, I can see where I got stuck this week. There's really no excuse; I'm choosing at this point. I have so many tools at my disposal to take care of these things. I really like the idea of blessing the hard stuff. I intuited that this week, I will stop resisting this. *I had another moment where I thought,* If I'm not allowing, I'm resisting, *which was suggested a couple of calls ago. This is keeping my choices front and center, and the things that might pull me off course are not distracting me. When they do, you can go "aha! Cheeseburger! I recognize you, I'm onto to you, and I will not be foiled! I've been here before, what do I do?" You recognize it and go,* I have the tools; I know how to get back into momentum and flow. *My challenges are not an external condition, and I don't need permission to shift my thinking! No license needed, as you said, to make more money; no doctor's note or permission from mom. This is all you—all your choice, free will and determined by you. It's a huge responsibility on one hand, but also freeing and exciting. It's an inside job literally.*

WENDY NOLIN:

It's not that we're powerless that scares us, it's that we have power that scares us. Because of this work, I'm just beginning to understand how much power I have in using it for the greater good of myself, and others. It's really what I see happening for me now as a result. I would say that's my biggest take away—I'm not just looking at this course as Prosperity for Writers, it's Prosperity for Everybody. It's been a very great reminder of how our power affects everything in our lives and just one of the things I'm doing is writing. It affects everyone around us, and everything, and we have the axis or power in order to do everything that we want. We have to understand how powerful we are, and wield the power safely.

CHRISTINA CULBERTSON:

It's important for me to reiterate day by day that you're right—I need to keep reaffirming and believing what I want and who I am. We are all children of abundance and desire only the best. If we see a situation as "negative" we have to step back and realize that we can't see the whole situation—our attitude affects our reality. By simply seeing the best in yourself, believing in your success, and being grateful for everything you already have, we create the best reality. Accessing gratitude will change your whole day or your whole week, and then you have to get back to it. These practices are a constant recommitment.

———

The beauty in this process is the fact that it is simple, it is free, and you can do it at any time. You can apply these ideas, tools, and principles to anything and everything in your writing life (better yet, to the rest of your life as well). You're going to learn in the next chapter the daily practices of prosperous writers, including how they overcome blocks and challenges so they can get the results they truly want. Before you can adopt and truly use them at the highest level possible, you need to have taken the time to define a new vision, and supporting beliefs. How about you do that now, and then keep reading? Turn the page, because that's where I'll be waiting.

HOMEWORK:

1. Identify your old money story and the beliefs that are the basis of that story.

2. How have those beliefs served you? How have they been a disservice to you?

3. Write a new vision for your writing business, the corresponding money story, and some awesome new beliefs that make you feel amazing!

6

PRACTICAL PRACTICES OF PROSPEROUS WRITERS

I had the honor and pleasure of interviewing some pretty incredible prosperous writers for this book. Some of them are practically household names—at the very least, those of us who write and publish for sure know who they are. Others you may only ever read about in this book. What they all have in common are practical, daily practices. As I mentioned before, it is tempting to think that someone more successful than we are is magical in some way. During my interviews,

I was curious to see if there was any validity to that assumption, and I am delighted to tell you there is not.

What I did discover is that they have several things in common: they work hard at their craft, they work smart, they work diligently at their marketing, and they are human beings just like you and me. The human being part was the most interesting to me because it meant that, no matter how long they had been writing, how many books they had published, or how much money they were making, they encountered huge challenges on their journeys to becoming prosperous writers. They helped me understand how they overcame and continue to overcome challenges as they pursue their current visions. I think you will find solace, comfort, and inspiration in what I am about to share with you in this chapter, so let's begin!

There are five core daily practices of prosperous writers, and not a one of them is magical or mysterious. In fact, you can discover them *and* begin to practice them—instantly.

PRACTICE #1: PROSPEROUS WRITERS WRITE DIRTY FIRST DRAFTS, AND THEY ARE OKAY WITH THE FACT THAT THEY ARE "DIRTY."

I love the term "dirty" when it comes to a first draft. What that means to me is I've completed the first piece of the project, and I still have the expectation there's quite a bit of time and effort that needs to go into polishing it—way before it becomes a final product. And I'm okay with that. Do you write dirty first drafts, or have you held yourself back from completing a project because you've tried to edit and rewrite instead of just finishing? Can you let go of an expectation of a perfect, final first draft (something that only exists in fairy tales and urban legends)? The real answer is a resounding yes— yes you can complete first drafts. Get those words down on paper. Any finished writing project wasn't written; it was *re*-written. Then it was edited, looked over, re-written, and proofread.

Your new practice of writing dirty first drafts includes making a commitment to yourself and perhaps your project. Finish this sentence, "I am committed to ____." Or, "I am committed to sitting down and writing my first draft by (date)." You could also make measurable progress toward that first draft by committing to a daily practice or goal, such as, "I am committed to writing 500 words daily," or whatever works for you.

PRACTICE #2: PROSPEROUS WRITERS WRITE EVERY SINGLE DAY.

They have a streak going, and they don't break their streak. Do you write every day? Maybe you don't at this point. Can you? Yes, I believe you can. Here is your commitment: *I am committed to writing every single day, to the extent it is not impractical for me to do so.* Have a streak if that works for you, or decide what you can commit to, and write an affirmation of that commitment.

I have been so inspired lately by Mat Morris, who is the cohost of the *Author Strong Podcast*. While I will probably never go on a 50,000 words-a-day writing binge, Mat has convinced me (and my subconscious mind) that I can write several thousand words every day. In a recent podcast, he shared that in one day he strives to write 5,000 words, the next day 2,000, the following day 5,000, and the following day 2,000. In just four days, he is able to write about 14,000 words! I thought I was doing a pretty good job writing 1,000 words a day, but my beliefs (and what's actually possible) have been altered by listening to Mat (and his very darling cohost, Nancy) talk about what really *is* possible.

The challenge with writing the words *daily* is the requirement to work in isolation. One way to overcome this challenge is to find writer friends, and listen to writer and author podcasts. Both of these will help you to get, and stay, inspired. Keep in mind that some writers write every weekday and enjoy taking the weekend to recharge their batteries. Find what works most effectively for you, commit to it, and do it.

PRACTICE #3: PROSPEROUS WRITERS MANAGE THEIR MONEY WITH FOCUS, INTENTION, AND ACTION.

How you manage your money is one of the more technical pieces of prosperity. What are you doing with the money you earn? How are you investing it? Are you manifesting more and more money? And when that money comes to you, how are you saving, investing, spending, and handling your money?

Are you doing what you need to do as a writer in order to produce regular work product? There must be an ongoing flow of work coming *from* you, so you can have an ongoing flow of money coming *to* you.

As I interviewed successful writers for this book and listened to podcast interviews with them and other successful writers, I heard time and again how they are mindful about their money. They are being good stewards of the money they already have. They are expecting new money to come to them on a consistent basis, and they know exactly what they are going to do with the money when it shows up. They know how much they are going to invest, spend, and save, and what happens to the money that's left over. They have plans for the money they know is coming in, and they have future plans to grow their writing business to make even more and more money.

In fact, they know how many books or articles they need to write and sell in order to earn a living from their writing. They actually put a number on it, and so should you! In your prosperity journal, write down exactly how much money you need to make on a yearly, monthly, weekly, and even daily basis. When you figure out you need to sell 23 books on KDP every day to earn more than enough money to live on, then you have something that's being measured. What gets measured, gets attention. What you put your attention on *grows*. You need to know exactly how much money you need to live on, without limits, and break it down into manageable, bite-sized pieces.

Be sure to apply abundance thinking to the amount of money you believe you need, instead of simply coming up with the minimum amount you need. Determine your monthly nut—i.e., what do your taxes, expenses, investments, insurance, food, overhead, etc., require? Take that number and multiply it by 1.5. If you need $10,000 a month to cover all of your expenses, shoot for an income of $15,000. You'll have an extra $5,000 to save or invest, or, if there is an opportunity that pops up, that extra cash will come in handy. Something might break, and you need to get it fixed. Either way, having more than enough puts you in a great position to both capitalize on opportunities and handle challenges with ease and less stress.

Focus on a daily number. Don't focus on exactly how much you need—focus on creating an abundance, and you will have an abundance. Your results will be based on what you're thinking and what you're expecting. It's not about having *just* enough; it's about having *more* than enough. Prosperous writers are rich by definition. They have more than enough, and that allows them to do more of what they love, which allows them to do more with it.

What are you committed to doing? Come up with your new intention for your money, and go about the business of generating that amount of money. The best way to do that is to make your affirmation statement. It's an interesting idea to play with, and it's interesting to watch it work.

PRACTICE #4: PROSPEROUS WRITERS MARKET LIKE THEY MEAN IT.

They are actively marketing their books and building their platform as though their lives and careers depend upon it (because they do). The most successful writers (and the writers who will become the most successful) have intention and purpose around marketing. Can you also market like you mean it? Of course you can! If others can figure out how to market themselves and their writing effectively, then you can as well. The marketing piece has been defined and expanded upon by fantastic people who are not shy about sharing their expertise. If marketing is a piece of the puzzle that is missing for you, you can figure it out by studying what successful and prosperous writers do. Then, use what they've learned for your benefit.

My favorite books on the subject include the aforementioned *Write. Publish. Repeat.* by Sean Platt and Johnny B. Truant; *Book Launch: How to Write, Market & Publish Your First Bestseller in Three Months or Less AND Use it to Start and Grow a Six Figure Business* by Chandler Bolt; *Business for Authors: How to Be an Author Entrepreneur* by Joanna Penn; *Let's Get Visible* by David Gaughran; and *Your First 1000 Copies* by Tim

Grahl. These books are my go-to reference manuals for defining and redefining my personal prosperity plan (which is coming up next). I highly suggest you purchase and read them, more than twice each, because there is literally millions of dollars of information contained within them (not to mention the time you'll save on your learning curve!).

Make a commitment to study marketing even as you study your craft of writing. In essence, while you're no longer in traditional school, you are most definitely in school, but the schooling is now only of your choice! It's up to you where to educate yourself for your own success.

PRACTICE #5: PROSPEROUS WRITERS USE CAREFULLY THOUGHT-OUT PLANS THAT MAKE THEIR WRITING AND PUBLISHING FASTER, EASIER, AND REQUIRE LESS EFFORT.

There are two plans you need right now: your Personal Prosperity Plan and your Short Term Massive Action (STMA) 100-Day Action Plan (which is an Honorée original). It is important to always have defined your plans and be working from those plans. Failing to plan is the same as planning to fail. Do yourself and your writing career a huge favor: take the time you need to craft two plans that inspire you.

The elements of your Personal Prosperity Plan include all of the work you've done up to this point—including the homework from each of the previous chapters and your goals for integrating all the practices in this chapter. I haven't created something formal, as in an official "Personal Prosperity Plan," but you may want to do so. Ultimately, you have to get exceedingly clear about where you want to go in a well-defined, concise plan. This plan will help you to crystallize all of the important aspects around your writing career and enable you to take the first steps forward.

Think about this: What is your plan for turning your writing into your main source of income? What is your plan for writing every single day? What is your first focus area in terms of managing your money with focus, intention, and care? How much is it you desire to earn? What is that number for you? You don't need to declare that number publicly, but you do need to ink it as part of your plan.

What is your plan for marketing? Nobody gets rich, or becomes a prosperous writer, by accident. Nobody gets rich from hoping. I do not believe hope is a strategy for anything. So, you'll put together your Personal Prosperity Plan and do you best to execute on that plan until you've achieved your goals.

In addition, there is one more formal plan that you may want to use, and that is my STMA 100-day Action Plan. You can find a free copy to download on my website: HonoreeCorder.com/resources (password: *success*). The STMA coaching program was born from my desire to be improving constantly and achieving the next level. Along with that, STMA gives you the opportunity for bigger and better goals. I wanted a way to track my progress easily and to continually improve my performance. Following is a quick overview of my Plan—you can read more in my book, *Vision to Reality.*

STMA 100-Day Action Plan

Because I didn't (and don't) prefer complex math, I decided to work in 100-day increments. Calendar quarters range in number from 88 to 92 days. In order to figure out where I was percent-to-goal, there was a whole lot of multiplying and dividing going on, and yes, that would be math.

Working in 100-day increments means that each day is 1 percent of my goal. Easy! For example, a goal to earn $10,000 in royalties could be divided equally and effortlessly tracked: 1 percent per day equals $100 per day. In addition, you can do the math to determine how many books would equal $100 per day. You know every day whether you are ahead, on track, or behind your goals based upon how many percentage points you have on a given day. On day 57, you should be at 57 percent of your goal (or higher), or $5,700. Or, you're behind and know exactly how much you need to catch up. You always know right where you are, and where you should be.

Your Plan consists of several important pieces:

- **Dates:** These are the dates of your 100 days. For example, Day 1 is January 1 through Day 100, April 10.

- **100-Day Vision:** This is your *what*. What do you want to accomplish, bring to fruition, and achieve over the next 100 days? Visualize it, and then describe it with total certainty and positive expectation.

- **100-Day Purpose:** This is your *why*. What would accomplishing your *what* give you? What would it provide for you, and help you achieve down the road?

- **Top Three Goals:** Make them SMART: Specific, Measurable, Attainable, Risky (at least a little), and Time-sensitive. The deadline for these goals is, of course, your 100th Day.

- **Empowering Descriptors:** This is the fun part of the serious business of goal-achievement. Give yourself a reputation, and live up to it. Use phrases that help you to turn on and rev up. My empowering descriptors include: *Marketing Master! Best book writer! Successful Authorpreneur!*

- **Three Areas of Focus:** These are the three areas of your business and life you want to focus on during the Program. They could include writing, publishing, marketing, advertising, weight loss (or gain), platform development, list building, etc.

- **Resources:** These are the people and things you can rely on to shorten your success cycle. They could include books, seminars, podcasts, conferences, music, mentors, coaches, programs, bosses, friends, and family.

- **Next Steps:** This is your data dump. Get out of your head and onto paper every single thing that needs to get done, whether or not it (a) has anything to do with your STMA or (b) has to be done by you (several of these things could be accomplished by an assistant). These items could include how many words you need to write to complete a project, the people you need to call, book covers that need to be designed, editors to be hired, cleaning out your car, buying cat food, or sending a birthday card to your mom. If you're carrying it around in your head, it's adding to your stress level and making you less effective. Take your list and put the items in order of importance. Your items will fall into one of four categories: Do, Delegate, Delay, or Dump. There is no limit to the number of items that go on this list. You will add to it over time, but as you add items, be sure to categorize them and treat them appropriately.

Steve Scott, author of more than 50 books, shared, "The hard work part is what we need to do. A lot of people get hung up on the products that are being sold for $2,000 that are supposed to be a shortcut—that they don't have to do the work, which is BS. I'm willing to do the work, and test what I've heard to see if it works for me. I look at what needs to get done during the day, I do my creative thinking while I'm exercising, and I know that if I put forth the effort, eventually the results I want will happen. I figured out from being in the military, and then having a 9-to-5 job, that I wanted to have complete control over my life, and I chose to start doing what I needed to do to make that happen. I knew I would make a lot of mistakes. I have embraced the fact that making a lot of mistakes would eventually mean I would get the success I wanted."

He went on, "It wasn't until my 14th book that I really saw success, results, and income. It doesn't happen overnight. There's a lot of effort that is put in behind the scenes that no one ever sees. I have a 60-part checklist. I don't go from idea to bestseller instantly; there's a lot that goes into my process."

Even seemingly overnight successes like Steve have put in thousands of hours of work before hitting it big and finding their way onto your radar. If you want mega success, you have to put in mega effort. Set that as your expectation, execute your plans daily and systematically, and before you know it, everything you want today will be yours.

My Thoughts on Challenges vs. Opportunities

If you are someone who believes "this writing thing had better work out," it may feel as though if you take a shot at it and fail, all will be lost. To that end, you may also feel like you're destined to fail. I have a different take on having only one shot at and option for success.

I know that some people who feel like they are in a desperate place also feel like they are at a disadvantage. But make no mistake; people who are in a good place can lose their edge and intensity. This can be its own challenge. If you don't have an internal drive, then you're not compelled to make something happen. If you don't *have* to get out of bed in the morning (perhaps, because you have a spouse who is a significant income earner), then you may not follow through because you don't actually have to. You then must figure out your *why*. If, right now, you're in a position that you have to figure out a way to make a living from your writing, or spend the rest of your life working in an unfulfilling career, you have the opportunity to channel that energy into doing exactly what you want to do!

When your back is to the wall, you have an advantage. You have fuel for your fire. If you're not clear on *why* you want your "what," then you may lose your drive. This is really important, not just because you could lose your drive, but because your drive could also be taken from you. You could jump the tracks for any number of reasons: sickness, death, whatever. Holidays get people off track. You have to be very clear about *why* you want what you want. That clarity will be the fuel that keeps your fire going. While you may feel like you're at a disadvantage, you actually have an advantage over someone who has lost his or her drive entirely. I see that situation as the biggest opportunity of all.

If you are now, or at any time, struggling there are a few additional practices that may come in handy. Within the first two weeks of participating in the Prosperity for Writers course, Wendy Nolin was in the flow and getting great results. Then, during the third week, it seemed like the wheels came off the bus. Prospects who seemed excited to hire her changed their minds. She got sick. She announced the release of her first book to a networking group, and no one bought a single copy. To say Wendy was deflated is an understatement. She shared her frustration and discontent on our third call, and after the call I reached out to her to give her some individual coaching. I shared with her that she needed to recommit to her intended outcomes every single day—every day she had to recommit to each thing that was important to her.

If you started doing some of the suggestions I've made in this book, you are going to get in the flow rather quickly. You'll notice abundance all around you, abundance coming to you, and perhaps feel like you're invincible. But at some point, if you feel like the flow has stopped, you'll want to take a step back and not only notice that the flow has let up, but recommit to the prosperity processes that worked for you in the first place. You'll see what you need to start doing again, or do more of, to keep the flow coming in your direction. To say it another way, at that point it would be time to turn on your RAS (noticing) and let the antennae go up—begin again to BOLO. There isn't really a reason to get out of the flow, but life happens, and at some point you might!

It's important to keep doing the practices that work. Practice doesn't make perfect, practice makes *permanent*. But in order for it to work, the practice has to continue ... and continue ... and continue. If you stop dieting and exercising, eventually you'll put on weight. Prosperity works the same way: you have to keep doing the things that work—and they only work while you're doing them.

My practice while I'm going through struggle is to literally walk around my house and say thank you for everything that I have. I scroll through my phone and give thanks for my friends, family, and connections. I think of all of the things I have to be grateful for, and soon the struggle doesn't seem so big ... or so bad. I don't know where you are on the continuum of feeling like you're in the midst of a struggle, and I don't know if you are having a struggle because there's a lesson for you to learn. It could be because it is 4 o'clock in the morning and it's always darkest before the dawn. The fastest way out of a struggle is to immediately shift your vibration towards gratitude.

What happens if you're in a dark place? You may need to sit down and write some words (and nobody is saying they have to be good words ... just words). You may have gotten out of the habit of doing your prosperity practices. You may need to review your plans. You may need to say your affirmations one thousand times, or at least until you feel much, much better. You may even need to review this book.

To stay prosperous, you have to develop, and keep, a prosperous writer mindset. This focused expansion in turn will expand into every other area of your life. Soon you will be able to capitalize on your initial momentum and quickly move forward.

HOMEWORK:

You know the drill: pull out your prosperity journal for this homework…

1. Commit to writing dirty first drafts. Write your commitment: "I am committed to:_____

    _____."

2. Commit to writing every single day. Write your commitment: "I am committed to:_____

    _____."

3. Commit to managing your money with focus, intention, and action. Write your commitment: "I am committed to:_____

_____."

4. Commit to marketing like you mean it! Write your commitment: "I am committed to:_____

_____

_____."

5. Commit to using carefully thought-out plans that make your writing and publishing faster, easier, and require less effort. Write your commitment: "I am committed to:_____

_____."

6. Practice gratitude.

7

ACCELERATE YOUR SUCCESS

You've stayed with me so far, and you're going to be thrilled you did! Now I'm going to share my super-secret strategies—the ones I use when I'm feeling lazy or worn out from being hyper-productive for weeks (or months) at a time and I'm ready for a break ... but I'm just not ready for a break in my income.

I'm going to talk about something I do, and you've probably heard of it (especially if you're ever gone to church in your life). But stay with me—promise you'll read the entire chapter, because if by chance you think I'm about to get all religious or church-y on you, I'm simply not. But, I am going to talk about tithing. The first super-secret success and prosperity practice is based on this basic principle: *If you want something, give it away.* I wondered, *what was the most important and best thing that I could share*—it always kept coming back to *giving.*

When I was putting together the Prosperity for Writers course, I went looking for information on tithing, but there is hardly any information on tithing for the nonreligious or the religion adverse. I was fairly surprised about that because I figured the principle of giving with a heart and mind for receiving surely would have been covered in non-religious terms by someone, somewhere. As one of my more religious friends pointed out, there wouldn't be anything on tithing from a nonreligous perspective because tithing has its basis in religion. Okay, fair enough. So, apparently this is it, right here: chapter 7 of *Prosperity for Writers*. *Smile.*

Everything I found on tithing sounded pretty much like this: *A portion of one's annual income contributed voluntarily or due as a tax, especially a contribution of one tenth of one's income for the support of the clergy or church.*

But when I started tithing, while it was a suggestion of both the Religious Science and Unity Churches I was attending at the time, I didn't take it to mean it was a tax. In fact, the way it was explained to me (in addition to the fact that it was Biblical) was that tithing was a way of showing yourself, your subconscious mind, and the universe at large that there is an unlimited amount of money in the world. Re-read that phrase: *there is an unlimited amount of money in the world.* And I believe you can have as much of it as you want. When you receive money, you give money ... and as long as you stay in the flow, you benefit from staying in the flow. Pretty cool, right?

The process of tithing for me is not about religion, a tax, or an obligation. I believe that tithing is a universal law and has been around as long as time. It is based on the premise that if you want something, anything at all, you have to first demonstrate you believe there's an abundance of it. And the best way to do that is to give it away. A tithe, which literally means "tenth," of your income is a fantastic place to start.

As I have given 10 percent of all I have earned, I have always had more than enough come back to me. I continue to give 10 percent of all I earn and I have, over time, noticed that sometimes as much as (or even more than) ten times the money comes back to me!

I was taught that we are *supposed* to give tithes where you receive your spiritual nourishment. If you are a religious or spiritual person, that is what I recommend you do. If you aren't a spiritual or religious person, then find somewhere to give a percentage of your income. Again, I suggest giving 10 percent to somewhere where you feel great about giving it. Wendy Nolin suggested in the Prosperity for Writers course that those who were looking for a nonreligious destination for their tithes could contribute to literacy programs, "Because we're writers, and writers need readers."

The very first way to demonstrate what you want more of (in this case money) is to find a place to give it away. This will prove to you and your subconscious mind, once and for all, you are abundant, come from a place of abundance, and always have more than enough.

MY SUPER-SECRET PROSPERITY PRACTICES FOR ACCELERATED SUCCESS

There are three things that I do every single day that you may want to do, in addition to the other things I've shared with you up to this point. They aren't practices I've ever really talked about, although I mention tithing briefly in *The Successful Single Mom*. I haven't mentioned these before because for a long time I thought they were too out there or woo woo for the average person. As *The Secret* book and movie took its place in our everyday culture, I began to feel more comfortable about sharing what I was *really* doing behind the scenes ... in addition to good old fashioned hard work, of course.

As discussed, the first practice is tithing. My weekly practice is to tally up all of my business income, and then write a check for 10 percent of the gross amount received. Almost every single week, the checks increase. For sure, every single month what I give increases, which means I'm making more and sharing more. This makes me very happy! Even though my businesses are shifting, expanding, and changing, I always receive more, and more than I need.

One of the promises of tithing (regardless of where you believe the promise came from) is that instead of straining and striving, as you tithe you will *thrive*. I suggest you look into the practice because I believe it is a super-secret practice that a lot of people do, but they don't necessarily talk about it. In fact, every so often I will casually mention, "I am a tither," and the person I'm talking to will say, "Me, too!" If the religious piece of it is not offensive to you, read the information that is available, and take whatever works for you ... and work it. I'm including it in this book because I really do believe the practice is magical, and it will work for you, regardless of your spiritual or religious beliefs.

A special note about being consistent and persistent: Just like diet and exercise only work when you practice them, tithing will only work as long as you are actually tithing. And just as going back to eating Oreos, pizza, and cheesecake once you reach your goal weight won't *keep* you at your goal weight, neither will abandoning the practice of tithing once the money starts flowing in. When I asked a Prosperity for Writers course participant if he was continuing to tithe just two months after the class, he said, "Here and there. Not consistently." I suggest committing and recommitting to all of the practices in the Prosperity for Writers course. But I neglected to specifically mention that tithing is one practice that must be given special attention and *must* be consistently practiced.

Here's why: you will almost immediately, usually within a week or two, see results from your new practice. And, even if you stop, for a time you will continue to see results from your new practice. But eventually the results dry up, and you're right back where you started. Just as you can go off your diet while on vacation, and lose 5 pounds … only to realize a week after getting home you didn't really lose weight, you actually gained it! What you experience in both instances is lag time. Just as it takes times to gain momentum, it also takes time to lose it. Do yourself a favor and once you start, just don't stop.

My second practice is saving. Just as I tithe 10 percent, I also save 10 percent. You may be thinking, *Oh my goodness … I was living on 100 percent of my income until fourteen paragraphs ago, and now I'm supposed to live on 80 percent?* All I can say is you definitely won't miss the money you tithe and save. The reason you won't miss the money you give away is because *it's coming back to you multiplied.* All you gotta do is BOLO for it, take note of it, and be thankful for it. Then, give away a portion of it, and the cycle starts all over again.

As a total bonus, those 10 percent increments you save are going to add up to a giant mountain of peace of mind, and much more quickly than you might think. Even $50 a week is $2600 a year, not including interest. Chances are you're going to make, and save, many multiples of that amount ... especially because of your tithing practice.

If you don't already have a practice of saving that is consistent, it is a really good practice to get into. Now is the perfect time to start, right as you being to tithe. Ultimately you will have a situation where you may want to capitalize on an opportunity and you'll want to have an *opportunity chest* (my name for a war chest), so you can write a check without blinking an eye. Or you will have a situation where you need money, and you will already have more than what you need in your opportunity chest. At some point in your life, you or someone you know is going to have an "oh no!" moment—you will need access to capital, and you will have it.

The final super-secret practice is a combination of using the power of visualization and saying affirmations. I am an avid practitioner of the Life S.A.V.E.R.S. practice from one of my favorite books, *The Miracle Morning*. Visualization and affirmation are the two practices I think are the most powerful and pertinent to the Prosperity for Writers process. If there's something you want to have happen, I encourage you to create a three-minute mental movie—including adding in the emotions for how you know you will feel after you get the desired results. How excited are you going to be when you have a launch party for your first or next book? How great will it feel to deposit the biggest check you've ever received from your writing—or get the largest direct deposit *ever* from Amazon? Visualize whatever your biggest goal is, and craft affirmations that you get a real positive kick out of saying out loud. These two practices combined are like rocket fuel for your intended results. You should also envision checks coming from random places on a consistent basis all the time. My visualization includes me receiving expected and unexpected checks all the time, and I do. Anything that you want to have happen, sit down and create your visualization of it. Then jot down an affirmation that serves you.

Affirmation examples:

- I love watching my sales grow day by day after I've released a new book.

- My book royalties increase month over month. I love being a full-time writer!

- Money comes to me every single day in multiple ways.

A Bonus Prosperity Practice: Put Everything in Order

I have another prosperity strategy that works wonders: get everything in your life in order. I don't know about you, but I find it hard to be my most creative and word-producing self when surrounded by clutter or disorganization. When my things are out of order, I feel like I'm out of order. It is hard to access our wells of creativity when we are distracted by clutter and piles of stuff.

I have one final two-part daily practice that will work wonders in your life (and ultimately in your checking account): the Vacuum Law of Prosperity. When you activate the Vacuum Law of Prosperity by getting organized and putting all of your belongings in order, you create a vacuum. Creating a vacuum means to establish space for something new to flow into your life. You can't put a new wardrobe into a fully-stuffed closet. You have to make room for your new items. You must make space for the new things you want to flow into your life … including money. Creating a vacuum allows for new, desired items to enter your reality— whether it is ideas, things, money, or gifts. Get your stuff in order: take the time to organize everything you own and have. By getting organized and getting rid of items you don't use, that aren't quite right for you, or no longer work, you will create space for more of what you do want. The following is exactly how to incorporate this practice into your life right now:

First, get your stuff, (everything you own and have) and every space you and your stuff occupy, in order. Clean up, organize, throw away, donate, and otherwise get rid of items you currently own that don't serve you or that you don't truly love. There is no sense in owning a bunch of clothes you don't wear (most people only wear about 20 percent of the items in their closets). Marie Kondo, in her popular book *The Life Changing Magic of Tidying Up*, encourages her readers to ask,

"Does this bring me joy?" If the answer is no, out it goes. I suggest you get rid of books you won't read again (you can always donate them to your local library, where they will patiently wait for you in case you need them; alternatively, you can buy a digital edition which will be at-the-ready in your pocket at any time). Things like papers you will never look at or need, dishes that get used once a year, and knick-knacks that are "too expensive to donate" should also be removed. The same goes for clothes, jewelry, shoes, purses, empty picture frames, extra sets of sheets … only *you* know what you're holding on to, so get busy getting your items in order. Bless and release anything that no longer serves you by throwing it away, donating it, or giving it to someone who will love it. You will then create the space for new and wonderful things to flow into your life–including money.

Finally, clear the clutter. Clutter includes what you have around you, and clutter can also be the words you say. If you don't have control over your entire environment, you can have control over *something*. Delete, erase, empty, purge, and remove. If you see a pile of papers, stacks of books or magazines, or surface areas that are cluttered and disorganized, add those to your list to put in order. These two acts alone, organizing and clearing, will make you feel lighter and more prosperous.

If you're overwhelmed at the thought of organizing every closet, drawer, countertop, and bookshelf, take heart. Start where you are, and remember Rome wasn't built in a day. Take consistent daily action until your spaces and places are organized. Then, step back and enjoy what you've created. The organized space you've created will give you inner and outer peace, which is truly a magnet for prosperity. Bonus: what you will notice next is that, as you are getting organized and getting things in order, you will become ridiculously productive, *amazingly creative.* Productivity is the predecessor to more wealth and abundance coming your way, and it will all start with a little straightening and organizing. Pretty great, right?

HOMEWORK:

1. Commit to a consistent, regular practice of tithing. Whether you give to a source of spiritual inspiration or to a charitable cause you believe in, make it a consistent practice.

2. Commit to saving 10 percent of your income.

3. Get your stuff in order. Schedule a couple of hours or a couple of hours per week for the next several weeks to get every single item you own cleaned and organized. You might even want to read *The Life Changing Magic of Tidying Up* by Marie Kondo.

YOUR TIME TO BE A PROSPEROUS WRITER IS NOW

Catherine Ponder, one of my prosperity mentors, is famous for saying, "Success is as much as 98 percent inner preparation, and only 2 percent outer action." As you can see from what I've shared in this book, your success and prosperity as a writer is a mental game. You have to play to win! Writing might be more than 2 percent outer action, yet I believe that once you master the mental side of becoming a prosperous writer, the world is truly your oyster.

I hope by now you've tried some of the action steps in this book. If you haven't, you, your book sales, and your bank account are in for a treat when you do. If you have tried some of the activities, then most likely you have stepped onto the path to becoming a prosperous writer. You may have even gotten some results! I encourage you to commit to, begin, or continue —a daily prosperity practice. This practice will inform and influence the results you get for as long as you are a writer. Create plans that get and keep you excited about your future while living in the present. Once you have stepped into momentum, do whatever you have to do to keep that momentum going.

Something I want to reiterate from the beginning of the book is that everything I suggest you do in this book *gives* you time. In other words, both the practical and prosperity practices will make your way easier—in addition to giving you more time, joy, and money. As I am ruthlessly protective of my time, I am the same with yours. I'm not giving you more items for your to-do list. My aim is to help you to gain clarity, peace, joy, and more of anything and everything else that you want— including more money.

It is up to you to make the connection between how you feel about yourself, your circumstances, and the actions you take to create them the way you want. As you work to improve your inside beliefs, and commit to and execute the daily actions you know will work, your results will continue to get better and better and better.

The final thing is to remember that you now have all these tools at your disposal. You can use them at any time, in any location, as much or as little as you like. Eventually, the only struggle that will exist is the one you choose, or find yourself in by default. By learning, adopting, and adapting the teachings in this book, you have been empowered and inspired to change and expand the way you think. You will notice and eradicate your beliefs as needed, and you have been given action steps you can take to prosper both internally and literally as a writer. Now you can go forth and earn a living from your writing!

Everyone that took the class commented that they could *feel* the amazing future that is coming. I hope you feel the same from reading this book. The future is great and bright, and it's yours to live as richly and prosperously as you can possibly imagine! I encourage you to start at the beginning of this book, this time with the intention of incorporating all of the practices in into your writing business and your whole life. Remember: these practices are meant to add to your life in more ways than just financial, and the more of your heart, soul, time, and energy you put into them, the more you'll get out of them. You have nothing to lose and everything to gain. I hope to see your name on the bestseller lists very, very soon.

Go forth and prosper and become a rich writer!

QUICK FAVOR

I'm wondering, did you enjoy this book?

First of all, thank you for reading my book! May I ask a quick favor?

Will you take a moment to leave an honest review for this book on Amazon? Reviews are the BEST way to help others purchase the book.

You can go to the link below and write your thoughts. I appreciate you!

HonoreeCorder.com/ProsperityReview

GRATITUDE

To my husband, fellow adventure seeker, partner, and best friend, Byron—I couldn't live my dreams without you.

To my amazing, smart and beautiful daughter, Lexi—I'm so grateful to be your mom.

To my fantastic assistant and angel-on-Earth, Christina–you are a blessing!

To the incredible individuals who made writing and publishing this book possible: the participants in the *Prosperity for Writers* course, my editing team Christina, Alyssa and Leslie, Christina for putting the book cover together, and Garrett for doing the layout … thank you, thank you!

WHO IS HONORÉE

HONORÉE CORDER is the author of dozens of books, including *You Must Write a Book, Vision to Reality, Prosperity for Writers, Business Dating, The Successful Single Mom* book series, *If Divorce is a Game, These are the Rules*, and *The Divorced Phoenix*. She is also Hal Elrod's business partner in *The Miracle Morning* book series. Honorée coaches business professionals, writers, and aspiring non-fiction authors who want to publish their books to bestseller status, create a platform, and develop multiple streams of income. She also does all sorts of other magical things, and her badassery is legendary. You can find out more at HonoreeCorder.com.

THE PROSPEROUS WRITER
BOOK SERIES

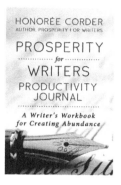
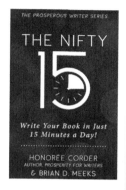

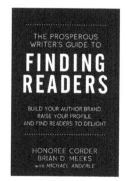

COMING SOON ...

The Prosperous Writer Mindset